THE STORY OF THE NEW TESTAMENT

THE UNIVERSITY OF CHICAGO PRESS
CHICAGO, ILLINOIS

———

THE BAKER AND TAYLOR COMPANY
NEW YORK

———

THE CAMBRIDGE UNIVERSITY PRESS
LONDON

THE MARUZEN-KABUSHIKI-KAISHA
TOKYO, OSAKA, KYOTO, FUKUOKA, SENDAI

THE MISSION BOOK COMPANY
SHANGHAI

THE
STORY OF THE NEW
TESTAMENT

By

EDGAR J. GOODSPEED

*Professor of Biblical and Patristic Greek in
The University of Chicago*

THE UNIVERSITY OF CHICAGO PRESS
CHICAGO, ILLINOIS

Composed and Printed By
The University of Chicago Press
Chicago, Illinois, U.S.A.

INTRODUCTION

It must always be remembered that Christianity did not spring from the New Testament but the New Testament from Christianity. Christianity did not begin as a religion of books but as a religion of spirit. There was neither time nor need to write books when the Lord Jesus was at the very doors. Still less was there need of authoritative books to guide men whose dominant conviction was that they had the Mind of Christ, the very Spirit of God, guiding them constantly from within.

But the ancient Christians did write. Situations arose that drew letters from them—letters of acknowledgment, thanks, criticism, recommendation, instruction, or advice. These letters, like our modern letters, were written to serve an immediate and pressing need. Situations arose which even drew forth books from these early Christians—books to save people from perplexities or mistakes, or to comfort them in anxiety or peril; but always books to serve some fairly definite circle, in a particular condition of stress or doubt. This practical and occasional character of the books of the New Testament can hardly be overemphasized, for it is only in the light of the situations that called them forth that these books can be really understood. Only when we put ourselves into the situation of those

Christianity is living! the best life possible. It is not a book.

for whom a given book of the New Testament was written do we begin to feel our oneness with them and to find the living worth in the book.

It may be helpful to conceive the writings of the New Testament as grouped about four notable events or movements: the Greek mission, that is, the evangelization of the gentile world; the fall of Jerusalem; the persecution of Domitian; and the rise of the early sects. The New Testament shows us the church first deep in its missionary enterprise, then seeking a religious explanation of contemporary history, then bracing itself in the midst of persecution, then plunged into controversy over its own beliefs.

The New Testament contains the bulk of that extraordinary literature precipitated by the Christian movement in the most interesting period of its development. Christianity began its world-career as a hope of Jesus' messianic return; it very soon became a permanent and organized church. The books of the New Testament show us those first eschatological expectations gradually accommodating themselves to conditions of permanent existence.

The historical study of the New Testament seeks to trace this movement of life and thought that lies back of the several books, and to relate the books to this development. It has yielded certain very definite positive results which are both inter-

esting and helpful. Through it these old books
recover something of the power of speech, and
begin to come to us with the accent and intona-
tion which they had for the readers for whom they
were originally written.

The short chapters of this book are designed to
present vividly and unconventionally the situations which called forth the several books or letters,
and the way in which each book or letter sought to
meet the special situation to which it was addressed.
These chapters naturally owe much to scholars like
Burton, Bacon, Scott, McGiffert, Moffatt, and
Harnack, who have done so much for the historical
understanding of the New Testament. But it is
hoped that a brief constructive presentation of the
background of each book without technicality or
elaboration may bring back particularly to intelligent laymen and young people the individuality
and vital interest of the writings of the New
Testament.

The purpose of this work is threefold: (1) The
book may be used as a basis for definite study of
the New Testament individually or in classes.
The Suggestions for Study are prepared for this
purpose. General and special bibliographies for
further reading will be found at the end of the
book. The student is advised not to attempt a
detailed investigation of specific parts of the various books, but to seek to get the large general aim

which controlled each individual writer. (2) It may be read as a continuous narrative, without regard to the Suggestions for Study at the close of each chapter. It will then afford exactly what its name implies, the story of the New Testament. The references to which the occasional superior numerals relate will be found at the beginning of the Suggestions for Study which follow each chapter. (3) After each chapter the corresponding book of the New Testament may be read, preferably at one sitting, and thus each piece of literature may make its own appeal on the basis of the introductory interpretation.

EDGAR J. GOODSPEED

CHICAGO
November 1, 1915

CONTENTS

xi

CHAPTER I

THE LETTERS TO THE THESSALONIANS

About the middle of the first century, in the Greek city of Corinth, a man sat down and wrote a letter. He had just received some very cheering news from friends of his, away in the north, about whom he had been very anxious, and he wrote to tell them of his relief at this news. As he wrote or dictated, his feelings led him to review his whole acquaintance with them, to tell them about his anxiety and how it had been relieved, and to try to help them in some of their perplexities, and before he closed he had written what we should call a long letter. And this is how our New Testament, and indeed all Christian literature, began. For the writer was Paul, and his friends were the people at Thessalonica whom he had interested in his doctrine that Jesus of Nazareth, who had been put to death in Jerusalem twenty years before, was the divine Messiah, and was to come again to judge the world.

Paul himself had believed this for a long time, and five or six years before he had set out to travel westward through the Roman Empire with this teaching. At first he had worked in Cyprus and Asia Minor, and it was only a few months before

1

that he with two friends had crossed from Asia to Europe and reached the soil of Greece. Paul was a whole-hearted, loyal friend, and he doubtless made friends everywhere for himself and his teaching; but he never made quite such friends as those who had gathered around him in these first months in Greece. At Philippi, where he stopped first and tried to interest people in his gospel, his friends made him come and live with them; and they thought so much of him that then and for years afterward they sent him money so that he might not have to work at his trade all the time but might have more opportunity to teach and spread his message.[1] The Thessalonians too had become staunch friends of Paul's. Some of them had risked their lives for him when they had known him only a few weeks, and others were to stand by him all through his life and to go with him long afterward, when he was taken, as a prisoner, from Caesarea to Rome. That was the kind of people in whom Paul had become so interested, and to whom he now wrote his letter. He had been welcomed by them when he first came to Thessalonica, and his very success among them had awakened jealousy and distrust on the part of others. At last Paul had been obliged to leave the city to prevent violence to himself and his friends. He had gone on westward along the Roman road to Beroea and later had turned south to Athens, but all the time he had been anxious about his friends at Thessalonica. What had happened to them? Had the opposition of their neighbors made them forget him and give up what he had taught them, or were they still loyal to him and his gospel? To go back and find out would have been perilous to him and probably to them also. So Paul had decided to send his young friend Timothy to seek them out and learn how matters stood. At the same time Paul's other companion, Silvanus, an older, more experienced man, had been sent on a similar errand to the more distant city of Philippi, and Paul, left all alone, had waited anxiously, first at Athens and then at Corinth, for news to come.

When at last it came, it was good news.[2] The Thessalonians had not forgotten Paul. They still stood by him and his gospel, in spite of all that their neighbors were saying against him. They still held their faith in Jesus as the divine Messiah and were eagerly waiting for his return from heaven, to reward and avenge them; and they were eager to see Paul again. So Paul came to write his letter to them. He wanted to tell them of his relief and delight at their faithfulness and loyalty, which filled his heart with gratitude. He wished also to refute some charges against his own work and character which people whom he had antagonized in Thessalonica had been making against him.[3] Then too Paul wished to tell his friends how much he had hoped to reach them, and how when this had proved impossible he had sent one of his two companions to them to find out all that he wished to know, and to give them encouragement and instruction; how he had waited for his messenger's return, and how he had at last come with his welcome news. But this was not all. Paul saw his opportunity to help his Thessalonian friends with their problems. Some of them were troubled at the death of friends, who would, they feared, thus miss the joy and glory of meeting the Lord Jesus on his return to the earth. Others were perplexed about the time of Jesus' return, and needed to be told not to trouble about it, but to live in constant readiness for it. Others were falling into idleness and dependence because of their confidence that the time was close at hand. Some needed to be reminded of the Christian insistence on purity and unselfishness of life. To all these people Paul sent messages of comfort, counsel, or encouragement, as their needs required. He was already deep in his new work at Corinth, in some respects the most absorbing and exacting he had ever done.[4] Yet he found time to keep in mind his Thessalonian friends and their problems, and to look out for them amid all his distractions at Corinth. Paul did it all, too, with a personal and affectionate tone, which shows how wholly he gave his affection to those with whom he worked.

We can imagine how eagerly the brethren at Thessalonica looked for Paul's letter and read and reread it when it came. They evidently put it away among their treasures, for that is probably how it came to be preserved to us. They certainly pondered over and discussed its contents; for before many weeks had passed Paul had to write them again more definitely about some of these things. Something Paul had said or written to them, or something they had read in the Old Testament, had made some of them think that the Day of the Lord had already come. Some of them had given up work, and were content to live in religious contemplation while their richer or more industrious brethren supported them. In their idleness some of them fell into unworthy ways of life and became a nuisance and a scandal to the church.

Paul was greatly stirred by this. He saw that it threatened the good name and the very existence of the church, and he at once wrote them another letter, our Second Thessalonians. It was a popular Jewish idea that in the last days the forces of evil would find embodiment in an individual of the tribe of Dan, who would make an impious attack upon God and his people but would fail and be destroyed by the Messiah. Paul in his letter appeals to this idea and points out that this great enemy has not yet appeared and so the Day of the

Lord cannot have come.⁵ There is therefore no
excuse for giving up the ordinary industry of life.
He reminds them of a precept he has given them
before: If anyone will not work, give him nothing
to eat. Those who refuse to obey this ultimatum
are to be practically dropped from the Christian
fellowship.

With these two short letters Paul began Christian literature. Before he ceased to teach the
churches he wrote more than one-fourth of what
is now included in the New Testament. But in
these first letters we see the difficulties that already
were besetting the small new groups of Christians,
and the patience, skill, and boldness with which
their founder looked after their development.

SUGGESTIONS FOR STUDY

1. *References:* ¹Phil. 4:15; ²I Thess. 3:6-8; ³I Thess.
2:1-12; ⁴Acts 18:1, 5; ⁵II Thess. 2:1-3.

2. For an account of the founding of the church at
Thessalonica read Acts 17:1-15.

3. Note the occasion of I Thess., 3:6-8, and the progress
already made by the gospel, 1:7, 8; 2:1.

4. Picture the receipt of I Thessalonians by the Thessalonian Christians, and read it aloud as they must have
done in a meeting of the church.

5. Note Paul's review of his success among them, 1:2—
2:1; his vigorous defense of his methods and motives as a
missionary, 2:1-12; his account of his feelings and movements after leaving them, 2:17—3:10; his moral teachings,
so necessary for gentile converts, 4:1-10; 5:8-23; his

commendation of labor and self-support, 4:10–12; the comfort he gives them about the Thessalonian dead, 4:13–18, and his reminder of the unexpectedness of the return of Jesus, 5:1–6.

6. Observe the prayerful and nobly moral tone of the letter, the intense personal affection Paul shows for his converts, 2:7–12, 17; 3:6–10, and the sanity of his practical advice, 4:11, 12; 5:12–14.

7. What facts about Jesus and what expectations about him does the letter reveal? 1:10; 2:15, 19; 4:14–17; 5:9, 10, 23.

8. Read II Thessalonians, noting its marked resemblance to I Thessalonians in many particulars: I Thess. 2:9 and II Thess. 3:8; I Thess. 3:11–13 and II Thess. 2:16, 17; I Thess. 1:1–7 and II Thess. 1:1–4; the sterner attitude toward the idlers, 3:6–15; the very Jewish argument in 2:1–10 that the Lawless One is not yet openly at work and therefore the Day of the Lord cannot have arrived; and the salutation written by Paul's own hand at the close, 3:17, 18.

CHAPTER II

THE LETTER TO THE GALATIANS

Upon returning to the shores of Syria after his long residence in Corinth, Paul had news that greatly disturbed him. An enemy had appeared in his rear. Among the people who had accepted his teaching about Jesus were many in the towns of central Asia Minor—Iconium, Derbe, Lystra, and Antioch. These places lay in what the Romans called Galatia, though that name included also an additional district lying farther north. They were in the region that has only recently been traversed by the new railway through Asia Minor. Their people had welcomed Paul as an apostle of Christ and had gladly accepted his message of faith, hope, and love.

But there had now come among them Christian teachers of Jewish birth, who looked upon the Christianity Paul presented as spurious and dangerous. Who these men were we have no way of knowing, but their idea of Christianity can easily be made out. They believed Jesus to be the completer of the agreement or covenant God had made with Abraham. In order to benefit by his gospel one must be an heir of Abraham, they held, and thus of God's agreement with him; that is, one

8

must be born a Jew or become one by accepting the rite of circumcision and being adopted into the Jewish people.[1]

There was certainly some reasonableness in this view. The men who held it were indignant that the Galatians should call themselves Christians without having first been circumcised and having thus acknowledged their adoption into the Jewish nation; and they considered Paul a wholly unauthorized person and no apostle at all, since he was not one of the twelve whom Jesus had called about him in Galilee twenty years before, nor even a representative of theirs. It was evidently the feeling of these new arrivals that the twelve apostles were the sole genuine authorities on Christianity and what might be taught under its name. This claim also seemed reasonable, and it made the Galatian believers wonder what Paul's relation was to these authorized leaders of the church, and why he had given them so imperfect an idea of the gospel. They admitted the justice of the claims of the new missionaries and set about conforming to their demands in order that they might be as good Christians as they knew how to be.

Where Paul first learned of this change in the beliefs of the Galatians is not certain, but very probably it was at Antioch in Syria, to which he returned from Corinth. He wished to proceed as soon as possible to Galatia to straighten matters out in person. For some reason he could not start at once, and so he wrote or dictated a letter in which he did his best to show the Galatian Christians their mistake. This he sent off immediately, probably intending to follow it in person as soon as he could do so.

The letter Paul wrote is the most vigorous and vehement that we have from his pen. It shows Paul to have been a powerful and original thinker, and is the more remarkable as it was written, not as a book or an essay, but simply as a personal letter, intended to save some of his friends from wrong views of religion. In opposition to the claims of the Jewish-Christian teachers from Palestine, he affirms with his very first words that he is an apostle, divinely commissioned, with an authority quite independent of that of the apostles at Jerusalem. This authority Paul bases on his own religious experience and convictions, in which he feels that the Spirit of God speaks to him; and this rightly seems to him the best, and indeed the only, kind of religious authority that really reaches the inner life.

The demand of the newcomers in Galatia that the Christians there should undertake some of the practices of the Jewish law, such as circumcision and the religious observance of certain days,[2] Paul denounces as unreasonable and dangerous. It is dangerous because if acknowledged it will surely

bring in after it the necessity of obeying all the
rest of the Jewish law, and will reduce the religious
life of the Galatians to the tedious observance of
countless religious forms.[3]   It is unreasonable because, even in the case of Abraham, long before
there was any Jewish law, faith, that is, an attitude
of trust in God and obedience to his will, was the
only thing that made men pleasing to God.[4]   It
was when the Galatians came into this attitude
of trust and dependence upon God that they felt
the presence of his spirit in their hearts as never
before, and in this fact Paul finds evidence of the
genuine worth of the gospel of faith that he has
preached to them.   The Law and the life of religious formalism which it brings with it can never
bring this consciousness, as Paul knows, for he
gave it a long trial before giving it up in despair
and turning to the gospel of faith, hope, and love.
In a word, the Law makes men slaves, the Gospel
makes them free.   This has been Paul's experience
and it is his teaching.

Galatians is in fact a charter of religious freedom.
Its noble ideal of the religious life, so far from being
outgrown, still beckons us forward, as it did those
obscure townsfolk of the Galatian uplands long ago.
Paul knew its dangers, but he knew its promise too,
and saw that for those who would sincerely accept
it, it opened possibilities of spiritual and moral development which could never be reached by the

lower path. The Christian had received the very Spirit of God. By that he must regulate his life. If he did so, he would be in no danger of gross and vulgar sin, but would find freely springing up in his life the fruit of the spirit: love, joy, peace, longsuffering, kindness, goodness, faithfulness, meekness, self-control.

This is the ringing message that Paul sent in hot haste to the Galatians. He usually dictated his letters to one of his companions, such as Titus or Tertius, writing only a line or two himself at the end. And this he probably did in this case, but emphasized it all, with a touch of humor, by writing his autograph lines in very large letters.[5] But some have thought that in his haste he wrote this entire letter with his own hand. It was carried by some trusty messenger away through the mountains to the nearest Galatian church and there read to the assembled brethren. Then they probably sent it on to the next town where there was a band of believers, and so it passed from one church to another until all had heard it. Some perhaps had the foresight to copy it before it was sent on its way, and so helped to preserve to later times Paul's first great letter.

SUGGESTIONS FOR STUDY

1. *References:* [1]Gal. 5:2–8; 6:12; [2]Gal. 4:10; [3]Gal. 5:3; [4]Gal. 3:6–9, 16, 17; [5]Gal. 6:11.

2. Read the account of the founding of the Galatian churches in Acts 13:13—14:28.

3. Note that Paul calls himself an apostle in the first words of Galatians as he has not done in Thessalonians. Why? Notice the occasion of the letter, 1:6, 7; 3:1.

4. Read the letter through continuously, noting the autobiographical chapters, 1, 2, in which Paul shows his practical independence of the Jerusalem leaders; the variety of arguments, chaps. 3, 4, by which Paul shows the folly of seeking salvation through the observance of law; and the stirring call to Christian freedom and life by the spirit which concludes the letter, chaps. 5, 6.

5. Read the letter through again, noting what you consider the particularly fine passages in it.

6. What does Paul mean by the "marks of Jesus," Gal. 6:17? Can these be the scars of such an experience as that related in Acts 14:19, which befell Paul in Galatia, or that in Acts 16:22, 23, which occurred after Paul's second visit to Galatia and before he wrote this letter? Cf. II. Cor. 11:24, 25. The figure refers to the owner's marks which were branded upon slaves.

CHAPTER III

THE FIRST LETTER TO THE CORINTHIANS

Paul had received a letter. Doubtless he received many, but with all his letter-writing we know definitely of only one letter that came to him. He was settled at Ephesus, working at his trade, and very much absorbed in explaining the gospel to everyone whom he could reach in that city and its neighborhood. Ephesus was a thriving center of life and industry, and people from the other cities on the Aegean were constantly coming and going. Among them were many from Corinth, which lay almost directly across from Ephesus, only a few days' sail away. Some of the Corinthian visitors to Ephesus were Christians, and others were acquainted with Paul's Christian friends at Corinth and brought him word of them.

Their news was not encouraging. The Corinthian believers, though they were probably few and humble in station, had divided into parties[1]. Some of them had begun to look down upon Paul as a man of inferior gifts, as compared with the eloquent Apollos, and of insignificant position in the Christian movement as compared with Cephas, that is, Peter. They had perhaps been visited by Jewish-Christian teachers from Jerusalem, for they were beginning to doubt Paul's right to be called an apostle.[2] Business disputes among them had led to lawsuits between Christian brethren in the pagan courts.[3] Worst of all, immoral conduct in the Corinthian church was reported to Paul, for the Corinthians had not yet fully learned that the Christian faith meant a new life of righteousness and love. With all these abuses the very existence of the little church was being endangered.

Paul was already troubled by these reports when three Greeks who had come over from Corinth sought out his lodgings and put into his hand a letter from the Christians of Corinth.[4] They had been Christians only a little while and had many things to learn. New situations were constantly coming up which they did not know how to meet. They had their social problems. What were they to do about marriage? Should they marry or remain single? Should a woman whose husband had not been converted continue to live with him? When they were invited out to dinner they might have served to them meat that had first been offered in sacrifice in some pagan temple. Was it right to eat such meat, and must they inquire about it before they ate it? Questions were arising about their public worship. What part were women to have in it, and how were they to behave and dress? Even the Lord's Supper was leading to excesses in eating and drinking and bringing out inequalities

and misunderstandings. The Corinthians were
much interested in spiritual gifts and their com-
parative worth. Some rated the ecstatic and unin-
telligible utterance which they called "speaking
with tongues" above prophesying or teaching.
Moreover, the persons endowed with these gifts
were so eager to be heard that the meetings were
becoming confused and disorderly.

On the whole the Corinthians were beset with
difficulties on all sides, and they wrote to Paul for
advice and instruction regarding their problems.
He had already written them a short letter about
some immoral practices that had appeared among
them or had held over from their heathen days.[5]
But that letter had not told them enough. They
wanted to learn more about the matter it dealt
with, and about a variety of other things.

So Paul came to write what we call First Corinthians. No wonder it is so varied and even
miscellaneous. Paul has first to set right the bad
practices that are creeping into the church—the
factions, the lawsuits, the immoralities—and to
defend himself against the criticisms that are being
circulated at Corinth. He attacks these abuses
with the utmost boldness. They must give up
their factions. Christ must not be divided. If
Paul preached to them a simple gospel, it is because their immaturity required it. And it was
such plain preaching, as they now consider it, that

converted them to a life of faith. The gross immoralities which Paul has heard of among them ought to make them humble and ashamed instead of boastful. Their lawsuits against one another disclose their unscrupulousness and self-seeking. Unrighteous men, Paul reminds them, will never enter the Kingdom of God.

From these painful matters Paul turns to the questions the Corinthians had asked in their letter.[6] Married people are not to separate, but the unmarried had better remain as they are. The offering of meat to idols is really meaningless and does the meat no harm, yet we have a duty to the consciences of others, and must not give them offense. When we are guests at a dinner, indeed, we should eat what is offered by our host without asking whether it has been offered to an idol. But in our freedom we are to remember to seek the good of one another.

In church meetings good order and modest behavior are to be the rule for both men and women. The Lord's Supper especially is to be observed in a serious and considerate way. More than any spiritual gifts Paul recommends faith, hope, and love as abiding virtues, much to be preferred to the spectacular and temporary endowments in which the Corinthians are so absorbed.

Some of the Corinthians had found difficulty with Paul's teaching about the resurrection, and

perhaps a question about it had been raised in
their letter to him. At all events, Paul comes last
of all to the resurrection, and defends his belief in
it in an impassioned argument, which rises at the
end into a paean of triumph.

So far has Paul brought his Corinthian corre-
spondents—from their petty disputes about their
favorite preachers to the serene heights of the
lyric on love and the vision of the resurrection. It
is instructive to see how he has done it. For he
has worked each of their principal difficulties
through with them, not to any rule or statute, but
to some great Christian principle which meets and
solves it. Nowhere does Paul appear as a more
patient and skilful teacher than in First Corinthians. And nowhere does the early church with
its faults and its problems rise before us so plainly
and clearly as here. Someone has said that Paul's
letters enable us to take the roof off the meeting-
places of the early Christians and look inside.
More than any other book of the New Testament
it is First Corinthians that does this.

SUGGESTIONS FOR STUDY

1. *References:* [1]I Cor. 1:10–12; [2]I Cor. 9:1, 2; [3]I Cor.
6:1–7; [4]I Cor. 7:1; 16:17; [5]I Cor. 5:9; [6]I Cor. 7:1.

2. Note that Paul had written to the Corinthians
before, 5:9. Observe the sources of his information about
matters in Corinth, 1:11; 7:1, and the occasion of the
letter, 7:1.

3. Note the immaturity of the Corinthian Christians, as illustrated by the evils Paul tries to correct—factions, fornication, lawsuits, chaps. 1–6. The Corinthians' letter evidently asked about the further topics of the letter, marriage, meats offered to idols, the Lord's Supper, spiritual gifts, and the resurrection, chaps. 7–15.

4. Observe the extraordinary variety of the letter's contents, in contrast to the unity of Galatians.

5. Read chap. 13, the prose poem on love, and note that Paul commends love as superior to the spiritual endowments which the Corinthians so overprize.

6. Consider the faults and perils with which the letter deals, as typical of the experiences of a young gentile church.

7. Notice how Paul works through problems put before him by the Corinthians to great Christian principles of life, 8:13; 13:13; cf. 6:19.

8. Note the beginnings of dissatisfaction with Paul in Corinth, reflected in 1:12, 13; 2:1–5; 3:1–6, 18; 4:1–5, 8–15.

CHAPTER IV

THE SECOND LETTER TO THE CORINTHIANS

First Corinthians was a failure. It has been so useful and popular in every other age of Christian history that it is hard to believe that it did not accomplish the main purpose for which it was written.

The factions in the church at Corinth, so far from sinking their differences and blending harmoniously into a unified church life, shifted just enough to unite all who for any reason objected to Paul, and then faced him and each other more rancorously than ever. His letters, they told one another, might put things strongly, but after all he was, when you actually met him, a man of ineffectual speech and insignificant presence.[1] The old doubt of his right to call himself an apostle still prevailed at Corinth. What right had he to set up his authority against that of Peter and the apostles at Jerusalem, who had been personal followers of Jesus in Galilee? If he were indeed the apostle he claimed to be, he would have expected the Corinthians to give him financial support during his stay among them.[2] His failure to do this suggested that he was none too sure of his ground.

While a few remained loyal to Paul, the majority of the Corinthians yielded to these views.

News of this state of things was not long in traveling across the Aegean and reaching Paul, and stirred him profoundly. Perhaps he went so far as to visit Corinth and face his accusers in person. But if he did so, he was not successful in meeting their doubts of him and restoring their confidence, and he must have returned to his work at Ephesus in the deepest discouragement. Yet he was in no mood to give up in defeat or to rest under the slanders of his enemies, and he made one final effort in a letter to regain his lost leadership at Corinth. This letter is what we know as the last four chapters of Second Corinthians.

The chief characteristic of Paul's letter is its boldness. So far from apologizing for himself, he boasts and glories in his authority, his endowments, and his achievements. In indignant resentment at their persistent misconstruing of his motives he fairly overwhelms them with a torrent of burning words. His authority, he declares, is quite equal to any demands they can put upon it; as the recognized apostle to the Gentiles he can without stretching his authority exercise it over them, and disobedience to it will bring vengeance when matters are settled up between them. Conscious that he is quite the equal of those "exceeding apostles," as he ironically calls them, whom the Corinthians quote against him, he warns the latter against the teaching of such apostolic emissaries.[3] His policy of self-support in Corinth was designed to save him from any suspicion of self-interest and to make the disinterestedness of his work perfectly unmistakable. The false apostles whom they are now following would find still more fault with him had he let the Corinthian church pay his expenses.

Foolish as boasting is, he will for once outboast his opponents. In purity of Jewish descent he is fully their equal, and in point of services, sufferings, and responsibilities as a missionary of Christ he is easily their superior.[4] More than this, in the matter of those ecstatic spiritual experiences, visions and revelations, which the early church considered the very highest credentials, he can boast, though it is not well to do so, of extraordinary ecstasies that he has experienced.

For all this foolish boasting they are responsible. They have forced him to it by their ingratitude. He has shown himself an apostle over and over again at Corinth, but they have not been satisfied with that. Now he is coming to them again, but not to live at their expense. He prefers to spend and to be spent for them; he and his messengers have asked nothing for themselves. He writes all this not for his own sake but for theirs. They must put aside their feuds and factions if they are to remain in Christ. Paul is coming again to Corinth, and this time he will not spare offenders against the peace of the church, but will exert the authority they have denied.

Paul dispatched this letter to Corinth by the hand of Titus. While waiting for news of its effect he busied himself with concluding his work at Ephesus. Days came and went, and it was time for Titus to return, but there was no news of him. Paul's thought went back again and again to the situation and the letter he had written in such distress. Had it been a mistake? He began to think so, and was sorry he had written it.[5] If it did not win the Corinthians, matters would not be the same as before; they would be much worse. If the breach was not healed by the letter, it would be widened. Paul was still full of these anxious thoughts when the time came to leave Ephesus. He had planned to go next to Troas, and now expected Titus to meet him there, but to his great disappointment Titus did not appear.[6] Conditions were favorable for undertaking missionary work in Troas, but Paul's anxiety would not let him stay, and he crossed the Aegean to Macedonia, still hoping to find Titus and learn the result of his mission to Corinth. There at length they met, and to his immense relief Paul learned of his messenger's success.[7] The Corinthians were convinced. Titus and the letter together had shown them their blunder. They realized that Paul was the apostle he claimed to be, and that his course toward them had been upright and honorable. In a powerful revulsion of feeling they were now directing their wrath against those who had led them to distrust and oppose Paul, and especially against one man who had been the leader of the opposition to him. They were eager to see Paul again in Corinth, to assure him of their renewed confidence and affection, and were even a little piqued that he had not already come.

Paul's relief and satisfaction found expression in another letter, the fourth and last of which we know that he wrote to Corinth. It constitutes the first nine chapters of Second Corinthians. He wishes to tell the Corinthians, now that they are ready to hear it, how much the controversy has cost him, and how great his relief is at the reconciliation. He acknowledges the extraordinary comfort which Titus' news has given him, coming as it has after the crushing anxiety of those last days at Ephesus. He is satisfied with their new attitude, only he does not wish them to misunderstand his continued absence. He had intended to visit Corinth on his way to Macedonia, but their relations were then too painful for a personal meeting, and he had put it off. When he leaves Macedonia, however, it will be to come to Corinth. He refers in a touching way to the anguish and sorrow in which he wrote his last letter to them, and to his purpose in writing it. His chief opponent whom they are now so loud in condemning must not be too harshly dealt with. Paul is ready to join them in forgiving him.[8]

Paul describes his anxious search for Titus and the relief he felt when at last he met him and heard his good news. He no longer needs to defend himself to the Corinthians, but he does set forth again, in a conciliatory tone, his ideals and methods in his ministry. In every part of this letter Paul shows that warm affection for the Corinthians which made his difference with them so painful to him.

Paul had been engaged for some time in organizing among his churches in Asia Minor and Greece the collection of money to be sent back to the Jerusalem Christians as a conciliatory token that the Greek churches felt indebted to them for the gospel. Such a gift Paul evidently hoped might help to reconcile the Jewish Christians of Jerusalem to the rapidly growing Greek wing of the church. In preparation for this the Macedonians have now set a noble example of liberality, and Paul seeks to stimulate them further by his report that the district to which Corinth belongs has had its money ready for a year past. He wishes the Corinthians to show the Macedonians that he has not been mistaken.[9]

It is natural to suppose that this painful chapter in Paul's correspondence with the Corinthians was

not put in circulation at once, perhaps not at all
while the men who were involved in it still lived.
The Corinthians could hardly have wished to pub-
lish the evidence of their own even temporary disloyalty to Paul, and visitors from other churches
probably had little desire to take home copies of a
correspondence so hotly personal. But toward the
end of the first century a letter from Rome revealed
to the Corinthians the high esteem which their
earlier letter from Paul enjoyed in the Roman
church, and this may have led them to collect and
put in circulation the rest of their letters from him.
In some such way, at any rate, these last letters to
Corinth were given forth together, but with the
letter of reconciliation first, to take the bitterness
off and commend the writing to the reader by the
fine note of comfort with which it begins. Second
Corinthians has never rivaled First Corinthians in
usefulness and influence, but no letter of Paul
throws more light upon his character and motives.
It is in these last letters to Corinth that we come
nearest to Paul's autobiography.

SUGGESTIONS FOR STUDY

1. *References:* [1]II Cor. 10:10; [2]II Cor. 11:7–9; [3]II Cor.
11:5, 13; [4]II Cor. 11:21–33; [5]II Cor. 2:4; 7:8; [6]II Cor.
2:12, 13; [7]II Cor. 7:5–7; [8]II Cor. 2:5–8; [9]II Cor. 9:1–5.

2. Read chaps. 10–13, noting the painful stage of the
controversy between Paul and the Corinthians reflected in
them.

3. What is the chief point at issue between them? 11:5, 13; 12:11–13; 13:3.

4. Note what Paul's Corinthian critics are saying about him, 10:1, 3, 10; 11:6, 7.

5. To whom does Paul refer in 12:2, 3?

6. How does this section, chaps. 10–13, fit the description of the third letter to Corinth given in II Cor. 2:2–4; 7:8, 9?

7. Note in contrast to it the tone of harmony and comfort that pervades chaps. 1–9, for example 1:3–7.

8. Note the occasion of this final letter, II Cor. 2:12, 13; 7:6, 7.

9. Observe the increased prominence of the collection for the saints, mentioned in I Cor. 16:1–4, and now again in II Cor., chaps. 8, 9.

CHAPTER V

THE LETTER TO THE ROMANS

Paul's work in the eastern world was done. For twenty-five years he had now been preaching the gospel in Asia Minor and Greece. His work had begun in Syria and Cilicia, then extended to Cyprus and Galatia, then to Macedonia and Achaea, and finally to Asia, as the Romans called the western-most province of Asia Minor. In most of these districts Paul had been a pioneer preacher and had addressed himself mainly to Gentiles, that is, Greeks. From Syria to the Adriatic this pioneer work among Greeks had now gone so far that the gospel might be expected to extend from the places already evangelized and soon to permeate the whole East. Already Paul was planning to transfer his work to Spain, where the gospel had not yet penetrated.

Between Paul in Corinth and his prospective field in the far west lay Rome, the center and me-tropolis of the Empire. Christianity had already found its way to Rome by obscure yet significant ways. Probably Jews and Greeks who had been converted in the East and had later removed to Rome, in search of better business conditions or the larger opportunities of the capital, had first

introduced the gospel there and organized little
house congregations. The fervor of the early believers was such that every convert was a missionary who spread the good news wherever he traveled.
The fact that Christianity was already established
in Rome helps us to understand how Paul could
think that Alexandria and Cyrene needed him less
than Spain, and to realize how many other Christian missionaries were at work at the same time
with Paul.

Paul was eager not only to occupy new ground
in Spain, but also to visit the Roman Christians on
his way and to have a part in shaping a church for
which he rightly anticipated an influential future.

One thing stood in the way of these plans. It
was the collection for Jerusalem. For some years
Paul had been organizing the beneficence of his
western churches, not to sustain wider missionary
campaigns but to conciliate the original believers
in Jerusalem.[1] The primitive Jewish-Christian
community seems rather to have resented the vio-
lent eagerness with which the Greeks poured into
the churches and, as it were, took the Kingdom of
God by force. The Jewish Christians were never
altogether satisfied with the way in which Paul and
his helpers offered the gospel to the Greeks, and
the growing strength of the Greek wing of the
church increased their suspicion. It had long since
been suggested to Paul that this suspicion might be

allayed by interesting his Greek converts in sup-
plying the wants of the needy Jewish Christians of
Jerusalem,[2] and he had already done something in
that direction. A more extensive measure of the
same sort was now in active preparation. The
gentile churches of four provinces, Galatia, Asia,
Macedonia, and Achaea, were uniting in it. For
nearly two years the Christians of these regions
had been setting apart each week what they could
give to this fund, and Second Corinthians shows
how Paul encouraged them to vie with one another
in this charitable work—a hint of the importance
the enterprise had to his mind. This collection for
Jerusalem has especial interest as the first united
financial effort on the part of any considerable
section of the ancient church.

The clearest evidence of the importance Paul
attached to this collection, however, is the fact
that he turned away for a time at least from Rome
and Spain in order to carry the money in person
to Jerusalem.[3] This can only mean that he felt
that the whole success of his effort would hinge on
the interpretation which its bearer put upon it
when he delivered the gift there. In the wrong
hands it might altogether fail of its conciliatory
purpose; only if its spiritual significance was tact-
fully brought out could it produce the desired effect
of reconciling the Jewish wing of the Christian
church to the gentile.

Compelled by this undertaking to give up for the time his plan of moving westward, Paul took at least the first step toward his new western program. He wrote a letter to the Roman Christians. The letter would at least inform them of his plans and interest, and so prepare the way for his coming. In it too Paul could embody his gospel, and so safeguard the Roman church from the legalistic and Judaistic forms of Christian teaching that had proved so dangerous in the East. And if this Jerusalem journey resulted in his imprisonment or even his death, as he and his friends feared, this might prove his only opportunity of giving to the Romans and through them to the people of the West the heart of his Christian message.

Righteousness is to the mind of Paul, as he reveals his thought in this letter, the universal need. Jews and Greeks are alike in need of it, for neither law nor wisdom can secure it. But the good news is that God has now through Christ revealed the true way to become righteous and so acceptable to him. This is accomplished through faith, which is not intellectual assent to this or that, but a relation of trustful and obedient dependence upon God, such as Abraham long ago exemplified. This relation is fully revealed through Christ, and the new way of righteousness has been confirmed and illumined by his death. Persons who adopt this attitude of faith are freed by it from sin and

from the tyranny of the law. The spirit of God
now dwells in them and makes them his sons, never
to be separated from his love.

In the failure of the Jews to accept the gospel
more than one early Christian thinker found a
serious problem. Was God unfaithful to his promises in his rejection of Israel? Would the Jews
never turn to the gospel? Paul explains the situation as due to the Jews' want of faith. They are
not ready to enter into the filial relation that Jesus
taught and represented. But their rejection of the
gospel and God's consequent rejection of them are
not in his opinion final. Some day they will turn
to the righteousness of faith.

This setting forth of Christian righteousness is
the longest sustained treatment of a single subject
in the letters of Paul. From it he passes in conclusion to instruct the Roman Christians upon their
practical duties to God, the church, the state, and
society in general. Few things are more striking in
these earliest Christian documents than their constant emphasis upon upright and ethical living. It
is interesting to find Paul urging his Roman brethren to be loyal citizens, respecting the authority of
the Roman Empire as divinely appointed, and the
friend and ally of the upright man.[4] The event
proved that in this he idealized the Roman state.
Yet, taking the situation as a whole, his counsel
was both wise and sound, for by virtue of it the

church, at grim cost indeed, outlived and lived
down the Empire's misunderstanding.

The letter to the Romans is often thought of as
the best single expression of Paul's theology. But
it is not less remarkable for its picture of himself.
In it he appears as the man of comprehensive mind,
not alienated from his own people, though he knows
that his life is not safe among them, actively concerned for the harmonizing of Greek and Jewish
Christianity, yet, even while engaged in a last
earnest effort to unite the eastern churches, eager
to have a hand in shaping the Roman church and
to reach out still farther to evangelize Spain. The
apostle is never more the statesman-missionary
than in the pages of Romans.

Many years after, when the Christians of Ephesus gathered together a collection of the letters of
Paul, a short personal letter written by him to
Ephesus from Corinth, probably at about the
time he wrote Romans, was appended to Romans
perhaps because, while it was hardly important
enough to be preserved as a separate letter, yet,
as something from the hand of Paul, the Ephesians wished to keep it with the rest. It was
written to introduce Phoebe of the church at Cen-
chreae, near Corinth, to Paul's old friends at
Ephesus, whither she was going on some errand.[5]
A Christian traveling about the Roman world on
business would find in many cities communities of

brethren ready to entertain and help him. The
value of this, in an age when the inns were often
places of evil character, can be imagined. Most
of all, Phoebe's letter of introduction discloses to
us the several little house congregations of which
the whole Christian strength of a great city like
Ephesus was made up in those early days when
the church was still in the house.

SUGGESTIONS FOR STUDY

1. *References:* [1]Rom. 1:15; 15:22–26; [2]Gal. 2:10; [3]Rom.
15:28; [4]Rom. 13:1–7; [5]Rom. 16:1.

2. Note Paul's circumstances and plans at the time of
writing Romans, as bearing upon its occasion, 1:8–15;
15:18–33.

3. Note the theme of the letter, 1:16, 17.

4. Observe Paul's argument, 1:18—3:20, that Jews and
Greeks are both in need of the salvation he describes.

5. Read 3:21—5:21, considering it as a description and
explanation of this new righteousness.

6. Read chaps. 7, 8, considering them as reflecting Paul's
personal experience in seeking righteousness through the
Jewish law.

7. Read chaps. 9–11, noting the difficulty Paul finds in
the Jews' rejection of the gospel (9:30, 31; 11:1), and his
hope that they will yet accept it.

8. Consider chap. 16: (1) As part of the letter to the
Romans: how can we explain so wide an acquaintance on
Paul's part with Roman Christians before he had visited
Rome? (2) As an independent letter introducing Phoebe
to some nearer church like that at Ephesus: how can we
explain in this case the letter's present position as part of
Romans?

9. Why does Romans stand first among the letters of
Paul, although it is far from being the oldest of them?

CHAPTER VI

THE LETTER TO THE PHILIPPIANS

Paul was a prisoner. His liberty was at an end. On the eve of a new missionary campaign in Spain and the West he had been arrested in Jerusalem and after a long detention sent under guard to Rome for trial. At the height of his efficiency the arm of the Roman Empire halted his career and changed the history of western Christianity before it was begun.

It would be difficult to overestimate the bitterness of Paul's disappointment. The great task of preaching the new gospel in western lands must go undone, or be left to men of far less power and vision, while the one man in all the world fittest for the task wore out his years in a dull and meaningless imprisonment. So it seems to us, and so at least at times it must have seemed to Paul.

Yet in his prison Paul had certain compensations. He could at least talk of the gospel to his guards, and through them reach a wider circle with his message. And he could keep in touch with his old friends and even make new ones by means of an occasional letter to Colossae or Philippi.

The first church Paul had founded in Europe was in the Macedonian city of Philippi, and the Philippians were among his oldest and truest friends. They did not forget him in his imprisonment. Hardly had his guards brought him to Rome when a man arrived from Philippi with funds for Paul's needs and the evident intention of staying with him to the end, whatever it might be. Nothing could have been more loyal or more practical. Ancient prisoners even more than modern ones needed money if their lot was not to be intolerably hard; and the presence at Rome of one more man to supply Paul's wants and do his errands must have been a great convenience to the apostle.

Unfortunately this man fell sick. Rome was never a healthful city, and we can easily imagine that his first summer there may have been too much for the Philippian Epaphroditus. His sickness of course interrupted his usefulness to Paul; indeed, it proved so serious and even dangerous that it greatly added to Paul's anxieties. When at length Epaphroditus recovered it was decided that he ought to return to Philippi, and to explain his return to the Philippians and make fresh acknowledgment of their generous behavior Paul wrote the letter that has immortalized them.

Paul had of course long since reported to the Philippians the arrival of Epaphroditus and acknowledged the gift he had brought. The news of Epaphroditus' illness too had gone back to Philippi, and worry over that fact, and a certain amount of homesickness besides, had added to the misfortunes of Epaphroditus.[1] As these facts put very kindly and sympathetically by Paul come out in the letter, we cannot escape the feeling that what Paul is writing is in part an apology for the return of Epaphroditus, who, the Philippians might well have thought, should not have left Rome as long as Paul had any need of him.[2]

Paul's letter exhibits from the start his cordial understanding with the Philippians. They are his partners in the great gospel enterprise. From the first day of his acquaintance with them they have been so. Again and again in his missionary travels they have sent him money, being the first church of which we have any knowledge which put money into Christian missions. But the Philippians did it quite as much for Paul their friend as for the missionary cause; for, when his missionary activity was interrupted, they continued and increased their gifts. Amid the divisions and differences— with Barnabas, Mark, Peter, the Jerusalem pillars, the Corinthians, the Galatians and their teachers —which attended the career of Paul, it is refreshing to find one church that never misunderstood him, but supported him loyally with men and money when he was at the height of his missionary preaching and when he was shut up in prison; one church that really appreciated Paul, and did itself the lasting honor of giving him its help.

Paul is able to tell the Philippians that his imprisonment has not checked the progress of the gospel preaching in the West. Not only has he been able to reach with his message many in the Praetorian guard and in that vast establishment of slaves, freedmen, and persons of every station known as the household of Caesar, but the very fact that he is in prison for his faith has given what little preaching he can still do added power, and inspired other Christians to preach more earnestly than ever. On the other hand, preachers of different views of Christianity have been spurred to new exertions now that their great opponent is off the field. So Paul's imprisonment is really furthering the preaching of the gospel, and he comforts himself in his inactivity with this reflection.

The Philippians are of course anxious to know what Paul's prospects are for a speedy trial and acquittal. He can only assure them of his own serenity and resignation. If he is to die and be with Christ, he is more than ready; but if there is still work for him to do for them and others, as he is confident there is, he will be with them again to help and cheer them. Meantime he plans to send Timothy to them to learn how they are, and he hopes shortly to be able to come himself. It would seem that while Paul's situation is still decidedly serious it is not altogether desperate.

With these references to his own prospects and the progress of the gospel in Rome, Paul combines a great deal of practical instruction. The Philippians are to cultivate joy, harmony, unselfishness, and love. In the midst of his letter[3] some chance event or sudden recollection brings to his mind the peril they are in from the ultra-Jewish Christian teachers who have so disturbed his work in Galatia and elsewhere, and he prolongs his letter to warn the Philippians against them.

Paul must have had occasion to write to the Philippians at least four times before Epaphroditus carried this letter back to them. Perhaps those earlier letters were less full and intimate, confining themselves closely to the business with which they dealt. Or perhaps it was the very fact that this was the last letter they ever received from Paul that made the Philippian church preserve and prize it. For out of his narrow prison and his own hard experience Paul had sent them one of his greatest expressions of the principle of the Christian life: "Brethren, whatsoever things are true, honorable, just, pure . . . . think on these things . . . . and the God of peace shall be with you."

SUGGESTIONS FOR STUDY

1. *References:* [1]Phil. 2:26; [2]Phil. 2:25, 29, 30; [3]Phil. 3:2.

2. Read the story of the founding of the Philippian church, Acts 16:11–40.

3. On what occasions did Paul probably write to the Philippians? Cf. 4:15, 16; II Cor. 11:9; Phil. 2:25; 4:10, 18.

4. Is 3:1 a reference to a former letter?

5. For Paul's experiences since writing to the Romans cf. Acts 20:4—28:28.

6. What effect had Paul's imprisonment had on the preaching of the gospel? Cf. 1:12-17.

7. How does Paul view the propagation of other types of Christian teaching? Cf. 1:18; 3:2-6.

8. Consider whether this letter is less logically organized than Romans, Galatians, or I Corinthians. How do you explain its informality of structure?

9. Notice the type of Christian living it commends, 2:1-18, and its frequent emphasis of joy.

10. Do we know of any other church which helped Paul with money for his own expenses besides that at Philippi? How often did the Philippians do this? Cf. 4:15-18; II Cor. 11:9.

11. What does the letter show as to Paul's own attitude toward his imprisonment and possible execution?

CHAPTER VII

THE LETTERS TO PHILEMON, TO THE COLOS-
SIANS, AND TO THE EPHESIANS

Of the many letters Paul must have written, only one that is purely personal has come down to us. It was sent by the hand of a runaway slave to his master, to whom Paul was sending him back.

During Paul's imprisonment at Rome he had become acquainted with a young man named Onesimus, who under his influence had become a Christian. In the course of their acquaintance Paul had learned his story. He had been a slave and had belonged to a certain Philemon, a resident of Colossae, and had run away from his master, probably taking with him in his flight money or valuables belonging to Philemon. He had found his way to Rome—for it seems that he had left Philemon in Colossae—and so had been brought by a strange providence within the reach of Paul's influence.

Paul's belief in the speedy return of Jesus made him attach little importance to freedom or servitude. He prevailed upon the slave to return to his master, and sent by him a letter to Philemon, whom he knew, at least by reputation, as a leading

Christian of Colossae. He asks Philemon to receive Onesimus, now his brother in Christ, as he
would receive Paul himself, and if Onesimus is in
Philemon's debt for something he may have stolen
from him, Paul undertakes to be personally responsible for it. Having thus prepared the way
for a reconciliation between Onesimus and his
master, Paul asks Philemon to prepare to entertain
the writer himself, as he hopes soon to be released,
and to revisit Asia.

While we may wonder at Paul's returning a
runaway slave to his master and thus counte-
nancing human slavery, it is noteworthy that he
sends him back no longer as a slave, but more than
a slave, a beloved brother. It was at the spirit of
slavery, not at the form of the institution, that
Paul struck in this shortest of his letters.

The letter to Philemon was not the only one
that Paul sent to Colossae at this time. There had
appeared in Rome a man named Epaphras, who
had been a Christian worker in Colossae and the
neighboring cities of Laodicea and Hierapolis.[1] It
was probably through him that Paul heard that
some of the Colossians had begun to think that a
higher stage of Christian experience could be at-
tained by worship of certain angelic beings and
communion with them than by mere faith in
Christ. They recognized the value of communion
with Christ, but only as an elementary stage in

this mystic initiation which they claimed to enjoy. It was only through communion with these beings or principles, they held, that one could rise to an experience of the divine fulness and so achieve the highest religious development. The advocates of this strange view were further distinguished by their scrupulous abstinence from certain articles of food and by their religious observance of certain days—Sabbaths, New Moons, and feasts. Their movement threatened not only to divide the Colossian church, by creating within it a caste or clique which held itself above its brethren, but to reduce Jesus from his true position in Christian experience to one subordinate to that of the imaginary beings of the Colossian speculations.

Paul had never visited Colossae. But his interest in Epaphras and in all Greek or gentile churches led him to undertake to correct the mistake of the Colossians. Still a prisoner at Rome, he could not visit Colossae and instruct the Christians there in person, but he could write a letter and send it to them by one of his helpers, who was also to conduct Onesimus back to his master Philemon.

Paul begins by mentioning the good report of the Colossian church which has reached him, and expressing his deep interest in its members. He proceeds to tell them of the ideal of spiritual development which he has for them, and takes occasion in connection with it to show them the pre-eminent

place of Christ in relation to the church. In him
is to be found all that divine fulness that some of
them have been seeking in fanciful speculations.
This is the gospel of which Paul has been a minister, especially to Gentiles like themselves. He
wishes them to realize his interest in them and in
their neighbors at Laodicea,[2] and his earnest desire
that they may find in Christ the satisfaction of all
their religious yearnings and aspirations.

As for the theosophic ideas which are being
taught among them, Paul warns the Colossians not
to be misled into trying to combine these with faith
in Christ. In Christ all the divine fulness is to be
found. They have no need to seek it elsewhere.
The ascetic and formal practices, "Handle not, nor
taste, nor touch," which are becoming fashionable
at Colossae, are likewise without religious value
and foreign to Christianity.

Over against these futile religious ideas and
practices, Paul urges the Colossians to seek the
things that are above. They are to live true and
upright lives, as people chosen of God should do.
The peace of Christ must rule in their hearts.
Wives, husbands, children, fathers, slaves, and
masters all have their special ways of service, but
everything is to be done in the name of the Lord
Jesus.

Paul says little about the state of his case.
Tychicus, who takes the letter to them, is to tell

them about that. An interesting group of his
friends is gathered about him in Rome, and in
closing the letter he adds their salutations to his
own. Epaphras, the founder of their church, Mark,
the cousin of Barnabas, and Luke, whom Paul here
calls the "beloved physician," are among the number. Paul sends an earnest exhortation to Archip-
pus, a Christian minister at Colossae, and asks
the Colossians to let the church in the neighboring
town of Laodicea read this letter, and to find an
opportunity to read a letter he is sending to Laodicea.[3]

What has become of this Laodicean letter?
Some ancient Christian writers identify it with the
letter we call Ephesians, and they may be right.
Perhaps the name of Ephesus has crept into the
salutation which begins the letter in place of Laodicea. Or perhaps the letter was sent to both
places, and Paul is asking the Colossians to get
hold of it when it comes to the nearer church at
Laodicea.

The appearance of such mistaken ideas among
the Christians of Colossae must have shown Paul
what low and inadequate notions many Christians
of Asia had of the spiritual significance of Christ.
It was evidently desirable to anticipate and prevent
the spread of these views by presenting a higher
conception of Christ's place and function in religious experience. This is probably what Paul

sought to do in the letter to the Laodiceans. It is clearly what he undertakes in the letter known to us as Ephesians. Every spiritual blessing, he tells his readers, is theirs in Christ. Through him they are adopted by God as sons. Redemption and forgiveness and the gift of the Holy Spirit they receive through Christ. Paul would have them realize the greatness and richness of the Christian salvation which God has wrought in Christ, whom he has made supreme. To this thought of the supremacy of Christ, Paul comes back repeatedly in the letter. He is deeply concerned to have them know in all its vast proportions —breadth and length and height and depth—the love of Christ, through which alone the human spirit can rise into the fulness of God.

Paul writes as one especially commissioned to the Greek world.[4] It is through Christ that the old separation of Jews from Greeks has been brought to an end, and the same great religious possibilities opened before both. As followers of Christ they must put away the old heathen ways and live pure, true, and Christlike lives. Wives and husbands, children and parents, slaves and masters are shown how they may find in the Christian life the elevation and perfection of these relationships.

Ephesians is very much like Colossians. This is not surprising, if it was written at the same time, to be sent by the same hand, to one or more of the churches in the region of Colossae; and we may think of Tychicus and Onesimus as carrying with them on their journey eastward at least three letters—one for the Christian brethren at Laodicea, one for those at Colossae, and one which Onesimus must with no little trepidation have presented at the door of his old Colossian master, Philemon.

SUGGESTIONS FOR STUDY

1. *References:* [1]Col. 1:7, 8; [2]Col. 2:1; [3]Col. 4:16; [4]Eph. 3:1, 2.

2. Read the letter to Philemon aloud, and imagine how that Christian gentleman, offended at the conduct of his slave, but full of love and respect for Paul, his friend and teacher, would feel and act toward Onesimus.

3. Note the letter's picture of primitive church life and the light it throws on Paul's character and on his attitude to slavery.

4. Compare the persons mentioned in Philem., vss. 1–3, 10, 23, 24, with those mentioned in Col. 1:1, 2; 4:7–17.

5. What are the ideas and practices criticized in Col., chap. 2?

6. What connection had Paul had with the Colossians, and how did he know of conditions among them? Cf. Col. 2:1; 1:3–8.

7. Note the resemblance of Ephesians to Colossians, comparing, e.g., the injunctions to wives, husbands, children, fathers, servants, and masters in Col. 3:18—4:1 with Eph. 5:22—6:9.

8. Does Eph. 3:2 sound as though it were written to Paul's old friends at Ephesus? Cf. Acts, chap. 19, and 20:17–38.

9. With the impersonal tone of Ephesians contrast Rom., chap. 16, with its numerous personal references and messages. Consider whether such messages would be likely to occur in a letter sent by Paul to the Ephesians alone.

10. To what letter does Paul refer in Eph. 3:3, 4?

11. How far was this new development in Paul's thought of Christ due to the problems which had arisen among the Christians of Asia and which Paul had to meet?

CHAPTER VIII

THE GOSPEL ACCORDING TO MARK

Peter was dead. The impulsive apostle who had followed Jesus about Galilee had lived to share in the world-wide gentile mission and had met his death in Rome. With him the chief link the Roman church had had with the earthly ministry of Jesus was gone. Western Christianity had lost its one great human document for the life of Jesus.

The familiar stories and reminiscences of Jesus' words and doings would no longer be heard from the lips of the chief apostle. East and West alike had heard them, but in the restless activity of the gentile mission, and especially in the general expectation of Jesus' speedy return, no one had thought to take them down. And so with Peter a priceless treasure of memorabilia of Jesus passed forever from the world.

But there still lived in Rome a younger man who had for some time attended the old apostle, and who, when Peter preached in his native Aramaic to little companies of Roman Christians, had stood at his side to translate his words into the Greek speech of his hearers. His name was Mark. In his youth he had gone with Paul and

Barnabas on their first missionary journey to Cyprus, but had disappointed and even offended Paul by withdrawing from the party when they had landed in Pamphylia and proposed to push on into the very center of Asia Minor.[1] He had afterward gone a second time to Cyprus with Barnabas, to whom he was closely related. Through the years that had passed since then he had probably kept in close touch with the Christian leaders at Antioch and at Jerusalem, where his mother's house had been from the first a center for the Christian community. It was probably as Peter's companion that he had made his way at length to Rome, and there until Peter's martyrdom had served the old apostle as his interpreter.

Mark saw at once the great loss the churches would sustain if Peter's recollections of Jesus perished, and at the same time he saw a way to preserve at least the best part of them for the comfort and instruction of the Roman believers. He had become so familiar with Peter's preaching, through his practice of translating it, that it was possible for him to remember and write down much that Peter had been wont to tell about his walks and talks with Jesus in Galilee and Jerusalem, more than thirty years before.

In this way Mark came to write what we call the Gospel of Mark. But Mark did not call it his Gospel; indeed it is not certain that he called it a gospel at all; and if he had thought of naming its author he would quite certainly have called it Peter's work rather than his own. But the order and the Greek dress of the Gospel are the work of Mark, however much he is indebted to his memory of Peter's sermons for the facts that he reports.

In the selection of what he should record, Mark was doubtless often influenced by the conditions and needs of the Roman Christians for whom he wrote. But it is Peter's picture of Jesus that he preserves, not of course just as Peter would have drawn it, yet with an oriental skill in story-telling which may be Peter's own. We see Jesus drawn by John's preaching from his home among the hills of Galilee, and accepting baptism at John's hands, and then immediately possessed with the Spirit of God and filled with a divine sense of his commission as God's anointed to establish God's Kingdom in the world. Yet he is silent until John's arrest and imprisonment, and only when John's work is thus cut short does he begin preaching in Galilee.[2] Marvelous cures accompany his preaching, and the Galileans soon throng about him wherever he goes. His freedom in dealing not only with Pharisaic tradition but also with the precepts of the Law itself soon brings him into conflict with the Pharisees, and their increasing opposition before long threatens his life. After one or two withdrawals from Galilee in search of

security or leisure to plan his course, Jesus at length
declares to his disciples his purpose of going up to
Jerusalem to the springtime feast of the Passover.
He warns them that the movement will cost him
his life, but declares that God will after all save
him and raise him up. Bewildered and alarmed,
they follow him through Peraea up to Jerusalem,
which he enters in triumph, now for the first
time declaring himself the Messiah by riding into
the city in the way in which Zechariah had said
the Messiah would enter it.[3] Jesus boldly enters the
temple and drives out of its courts the privileged
dealers in sacrificial victims who had made it their
market-place. The Sadducees, who control the
temple and profit by these abuses, on the night of
the Passover have him arrested, and after hasty
examinations before Jewish and Roman authorities hurry him the next morning to execution. Up
to the very hour of his arrest, Jesus does not give
up all hope of succeeding in Jerusalem and win-
ning the nation to his teaching of the presence of
the Kingdom of God on the earth.[4] The book
more than once predicts his resurrection; and in
its complete form it doubtless contained a brief
account of his appearance to the two Marys and
Salome after his burial; but it had by the beginning of the second century lost its original end-
ing, and while two conclusions have been used in
different manuscripts to complete it, the original

one, probably only ten or twelve lines long, has never been certainly restored.

Informal and unambitious as Mark's gospel narrative is, and lightly as it was esteemed in the ancient church, in comparison with the richer works of Matthew and Luke, no more convincing or dramatic account has been written of the sublime and heroic effort of Jesus to execute the greatest task ever conceived by man—to set up the Kingdom of God on earth.

SUGGESTIONS FOR STUDY

1. *References:* [1]Acts 13:13; 15:37–40; [2]Mark 1:14; [3]Zech. 9:9; [4]Mark 14:34–36.

2. Read the Gospel of Mark, noting that it consists for the most part of short units of narrative embodying some crisp saying of Jesus.

3. Judging from Mark alone, how much time would you say its action covered?

4. Observe the expectation of a reappearance of Jesus in Galilee that appears in the Gospel (14:28; 16:7), but is not satisfied in the present conclusion, 16:9–20.

5. Consider how welcome this Gospel must have been to Christians who had before had no written record of Jesus' life or ministry.

6. Is it probable that Peter, in the selection of what he should relate about Jesus in his sermons, was influenced by the needs and problems of his hearers?

7. Is it probable that Mark was guided in part in the choice of what he should include in his Gospel by the situation and conditions of the Roman Christians?

8. How long would it have taken Jesus to utter those sayings of his which Mark preserves?

9. Note the large part played by wonders of healing, feeding, etc., in Mark, and the usually beneficent character of these.

10. What wonders recorded in the Old Testament are most like those of Jesus which Mark reports? Cf. I Kings, chap. 17—II Kings, chap. 2; II Kings, chaps. 2–13.

11. Consider whether the marvelous is peculiar to the New Testament or whether it appears in contemporary Greco-Roman literature—Suetonius, Tacitus, etc.—as well.

12. Do you find much theology in Mark?

13. Does Mark regard Jesus as the Christ? Does Jesus so describe himself in this Gospel? What does he mean by "Son of Man"?

CHAPTER IX

THE GOSPEL ACCORDING TO MATTHEW

The Christian movement had failed in its first campaign. The nation in which it had arisen and to which its founder belonged had disowned it. It was as though the Israelites had refused Moses. This was the more staggering because the gospel had been represented by Jesus' early followers as the crown and completion of Judaism. Jesus was to be the Jewish Messiah, through whom the nation's high hopes of spiritual triumph were to be realized. But the Jews had refused to recognize in him the long-expected deliverer, and had disclaimed his gospel. Who was right? The prophets had anticipated a redeemed and glorified nation, but the nation had refused to be redeemed and glorified by such a Messiah. The divine program had broken down.

Yet the gospel was not failing. Among the Greeks of the Roman Empire it was having large and increasing success. Strangers were taking the places which the prophets had expected would be occupied by their own Jewish countrymen. The church was rapidly becoming a Greek affair. The Gentiles had readily accepted the Messiah and made him their own. To a Christian thinker of

Jewish training this only increased the difficulty of the problem. For how could the messiahship of Jesus be harmonized with the nation's rejection of him? The prophets had associated the messianic deliverer with the redeemed nation, but the event of history had disappointed this hope. What did it mean? Were the prophets wrong, or was Jesus not the Messiah? Paul had seen the difficulty, and in writing to the Romans had proposed a solution. It was in effect that the Jews would ultimately turn to the gospel, and so all Israel would be saved. Yet since the writing of Romans the breach between Jews and Christians had widened, and Paul's solution seemed more improbable than ever.

But an event had now happened which put a new aspect on the matter. Jerusalem had fallen. The downfall of the Jewish nation put into the hand of the evangelist the key to the mystery. Jesus was the Messiah of the prophets. He had offered the Kingdom of Heaven to the Jews, finally presenting himself as Messiah before the assembled nation in its capital at its great annual feast. Misled by its religious leaders, the nation had rejected him and driven him to his death. But in this rejection it had condemned itself. God had rejected Israel and the kingdom it had disowned had been given to the nations. In the fall of Jerusalem the evangelist saw the punishment of the Jewish nation for its rejection of the Messiah, and in this fact the proof that the gospel was intended for all nations.

The vehicle for this trenchant and timely philosophy of early Christian history was to be a book. It may be called the first book of Christian literature, for Paul's writings, great as they are, are letters, not books, and Mark for all its value is hardly to be dignified as a book, in the sense of a conscious literary creation. This book was to be a life of the Messiah, which should articulate the gospel with the Jewish scriptures and legitimize the Christian movement. For this purpose a variety of materials lay ready to the evangelist's hand. The narrative we know as Mark was familiar to him. He had also a collection of Jesus' sayings in Aramaic, probably from the hand of the apostle Matthew, and one or two other primitive documents of mingled discourse and incident. The mere possession of these partial and unrelated writings was in itself a challenge to harmonize and even combine them, just as our Four Gospels have ever since their origin invited the harmonist and the biographer.

With a freedom and a skill that are alike surprising, the evangelist has wrought these materials into the first life of Christ. Perhaps it might better be called the first historic apology for universal Christianity. For it is a biography with a purpose. Jesus, though legally descended from Abraham

through the royal line of David, is really begotten of
the Holy Spirit, a symbol at once of his sinlessness
and his sonship. Divinely acknowledged as Messiah at his baptism, and victorious over Satan in
the temptation conflict, he declares his message in
a series of great sermons, setting forth in each
some notable aspect of the Kingdom of Heaven.
In the first of these, the Sermon on the Mount,
Jesus demands of those who would enter the new
Kingdom a righteousness higher than that based
by the scribes upon the Jewish law, and he follows
this bold demand with a series of prophetic and
messianic acts which show his right to make it.
The Jewish leaders are unconvinced and quickly
become hostile. His nearest disciples at length
recognize in him the Messiah, and he welcomes
this expression of their faith.[1] Soon afterward
they gain a new idea of the spiritual and prophetic
character of his messiahship through the transfiguration experience, in which they see him associated with Moses and Elijah, the great prophetic
molders of the Jewish religion.

Already foreseeing the fatal end of his work,
Jesus yet continues to preach in Galilee, and at length
sets out for Jerusalem to put the nation to the
supreme test of accepting or refusing his message.
They refuse it, and he predicts the nation's doom
in consequence. The Kingdom of God shall be
taken away from them and given to a nation

that brings forth the fruits thereof.[2]   The last discourses denounce the wickedness and hypocrisy of
the nation's religious leaders, and pronounce the
doom of the city and nation, to be followed shortly
by the triumphant return of the Messiah in judgment. The Jewish leaders, offended at his claims
of authority, cause his arrest and execution. Yet
on the third day he reappears to some women of
the disciples' company, and afterward to the disciples on a mountain in Galilee, when he charges
them to carry his gospel to all the nations.

Jesus had expressly confined his own work and
that of his disciples, during his life, to the Jews,
but since they had refused the gospel, his last command to his followers was to offer it henceforth
to all mankind.

The Jewish war of 66–70 A.D., culminating in
the fall of Jerusalem and the destruction of the
last vestige of Jewish national life, must have
brought what Jesus had said of these things power-
fully before his followers' minds, and shown them a
welcome solution for the problem that perplexed
them. Jesus had not come to destroy Law or
prophets; his work and its fortunes stood in close
relation with them. But as between the Jewish
Messiah and the Jewish nation, the verdict of history had gone for the Messiah and against the
nation, for the nation had already perished while
he was worshiped by half the world.

The obviousness of this solution to our minds is simply an evidence of the evangelist's success in grappling with the problem; for we owe to him the solution that seems so simple and complete. Few any longer stop to think that a triumphant Messiah apart from a triumphant nation is hardly hinted at in the Old Testament. In this as in other respects the success of the book was early and lasting. As a life of the Messiah it swept aside all the partial documents its author had used as his sources. Most of them perished—among them the priceless Sayings by Matthew the apostle— probably because the evangelist had wrought into his book everything of evident worth that they contained. Even what we call the Gospel of Mark seems by the narrowest margin to have escaped destruction through neglect, and its escape is the more to be wondered at since practically all that it offered to the religious life of the early church had been taken up into this new life of Christ.

For the probably Jewish-Christian circle for which it was written the new book performed a threefold task. It solved, by its philosophy of Christian history, their most serious intellectual problem. It harmonized and unified their diverse materials relating to Jesus' life and teaching. And it did these things with an intuitive sense for religious values that has given it its unique position

ever since. Forty years after it was written it
was quoted at Antioch as "the Gospel," being
probably the first book to bear that name. Twenty
years later, when the Ephesian leaders for some
reason put together the Four Gospels, the first
place among them was given to it, and its name
was extended to the whole group. A new desig-
nation had therefore to be found for it, and it was
distinguished as "according to Matthew," probably in recognition of that apostolic record which
it alone embodied. Of its actual author, however,
we know only that he was a Jewish Christian of
insight and devotion, who preferred to remain unknown, and cared only to exalt the figure of Jesus,
the Son of Man and the Son of God.

SUGGESTIONS FOR STUDY

1. *References:* [1] Matt. 16:15–17; [2] Matt. 21:43.

2. In what respects is the scope of Matthew wider than
that of Mark?

3. Note the great discourses characteristic of Matt.,
chaps. 5–7, 10, 13, 18, 23–25.

4. Note that practically all of Mark (all but perhaps 40
verses) is taken over into Matthew. Can you think of
any reason for Matthew's omitting Mark 7:3, 4; 8:22–26;
12:32–34?

5. Compare Matt. 16:13–20 with Mark 8:27–30, noting
how Jesus' reticence about his messiahship disappears in
Matthew.

6. Compare Matt. 21:19 with Mark 11:20. What is
the effect of Matthew's way of telling the story?

7. Notice the repeated emphasis on the fulfilment of prophecy, 1:22; 2:15, 17, 23; 4:14; 8:17; 12:17; 13:35; 21:4; 26:56; 27:9. How does this relate to the purposes of the Gospel?

8. Notice the Beatitudes, the Lord's Prayer, and the great parables of Matthew.

9. Consider whether Matthew is richer than Mark (1) theologically, (2) historically, (3) religiously.

CHAPTER X

THE GOSPEL ACCORDING TO LUKE

The acts and sayings of Jesus seem from the earliest times to have been taught by Christian missionaries to their converts, and by these in turn to those who afterward became Christians. Paul reminds the Corinthians how he had delivered unto them what he had himself received as to the Last Supper,[1] and the death, burial, and resurrection of Jesus.[2] Paul had been taught these things after his conversion, and he was accustomed to tell them to his converts. In this way the principal facts of what we call the gospel story became known to all Christian believers.

But the story was not always the same. Scores of missionaries were at work about the eastern Mediterranean, but not all of them had been taught the gospel story by Paul or by the men who had taught him. The Christians who fled from Judaea when the persecution in connection with Stephen's work arose, and who carried the gospel into various parts of the eastern world, probably did not tell their converts precisely the same series of acts and sayings of Jesus. After these early missionaries had left Judaea, new stories and sayings about Jesus' work must have come out as the value of

such memories became more evident. Here and
there people took the trouble to write down these
stories for their own instruction and enjoyment or
for use in their missionary work.   Fifty years after
Jesus' death there had in these ways arisen a
variety of partial accounts of his birth, his ministry, and his death and resurrection, which to a
thoughtful mind must have been very perplexing.

It was this perplexity that led Paul's friend
Luke, a Greek physician living somewhere on the
shores of the Aegean Sea, to write his Gospel. With
this confusion of partial narratives and oral tradition intelligent Greek Christians hardly knew what
to believe about the life and teaching of Jesus. One
such at least, a certain Theophilus, a man of position and intelligence, was a friend of Luke's, and
perhaps suggested to him his perplexity and what
ought to be done to relieve it. For him and for
the growing class of intelligent Christian people
Luke undertook to bring together into one comprehensive and orderly record what was most valuable in the tradition and narratives which had
sprung up in various parts of the world.[3]

Luke traces the ancestry of Jesus not simply to
David and Abraham, but back to Adam the son of
God, thus emphasizing his human nature more
than his Jewish blood, and preparing the way for
his later emphasis on the universal elements in
Jesus' ministry. At the same time he declares

Jesus to be in a special and immediate sense the child of the Holy Spirit. The consciousness that he is God's son attends Jesus even in his youth, when after a visit to Jerusalem he lingers in the temple, calling it his Father's house.[4] At the very outset of his ministry Jesus appears in the synagogue at Nazareth and declares that Isaiah's prophecy of a Messiah with good tidings for the poor and wretched is fulfilled in him.[5] In the spirit of this prophecy Jesus, though rejected by his townspeople, goes to Capernaum and by his cures and teaching achieves an immediate success. Four fishermen of the neighborhood become his followers. He goes about Galilee teaching the people and healing the sick and demon-possessed. His disregard of scribal precepts and his claim that he has power to forgive sins offend the Pharisees, and they begin to plot against him. He calls twelve men to him to be his apostles, and in a great sermon explains to his disciples the moral spirit which should govern their lives.[6] Accompanied by the Twelve he continues to travel about Galilee, teaching and healing, and even restoring dead persons to life. The Twelve, who have now seen something of his work and spirit, are sent forth through the country to heal the sick and cast out demons and to proclaim the coming of the Kingdom of God.

On their return Jesus feeds a multitude with a few loaves, and afterward asks the disciples who

the people think him to be. They give various
answers, but Peter pronounces him the Messiah.
Jesus charges them to keep this to themselves, and
tells them that rejection and death lie before him,
but that the Kingdom of God will soon come. The
transfiguration gives his closest intimates a better
idea of the kind of Messiah he is to be, and he again
foretells his death and resurrection.

At length Jesus sets forth on the momentous
journey to Jerusalem, sending messengers before
him to make ready for his coming in the villages
through which he is to pass.[7] Teaching and healing
as he goes, he is more than once entertained by
Pharisees, and on one occasion is warned by them
of the danger threatening him from Herod; but
he only grows more earnest in his warnings against
them. In the parables of the Lost Sheep, the Lost
Coin, and the Lost Son, he defends his course in
associating with sinners, that is, persons who did
not fully observe the Jewish law. As he approaches
Jerusalem, he reminds the Twelve that death and
resurrection await him there. Reaching the city he
enters it in messianic state amid the acclamations
of the people. He goes into the temple and clears
it of the traders who use its courts for their traffic.
The Jewish leaders protest and demand his authority for this act. His answer does not satisfy
them and they prepare to kill him. But he teaches
daily in the temple, already crowded with those

who had come up for the feast of the Passover,
and in the parable of the Vineyard he sets forth
the peril of the nation in rejecting and destroying
him. After a series of clashes with Pharisees and
Sadducees, he foretells the destruction of Jerusalem, the coming of the Kingdom of God, and the
return of the Messiah on the clouds of heaven. He
eats the Passover supper with his disciples, and
immediately after is arrested in a garden on the
Mount of Olives. After a series of examinations
before the high priest, the Jewish council, the
Roman procurator, and Herod, the tetrarch of
Galilee, who is in the city, and although neither
Pilate nor Herod find him guilty, he is condemned
and crucified. Immediately after the Sabbath,
however, he appears, first to two of his disciples,
then to the eleven apostles and their company in
Jerusalem. He reminds them that all this has
been in accord with the Scriptures, declares that
repentance and forgiveness are to be preached in his
name to all nations, and is taken from them into
heaven.

More than any other evangelist Luke claims to
have a historical purpose. His aim is to acquaint
himself with all the sources, oral and written, for
his work, and to set forth in order the results he
ascertains. It is this historical aim that leads him
to fix the date of Jesus' birth by the Augustan
enrolment under Quirinius, to date the appearance

of John the Baptist in the fifteenth year of Tiberius, and to tell us how old Jesus was when he began to preach. He is the only writer in the New Testament who sees the need of such particulars and tries to supply them.

Luke is evidently a Greek writing for Greeks. The fate of the Jewish nation interests him less than the universal elements in Jesus' work. The stories of Jesus seeking hospitality in a Samaritan village, of the good Samaritan, and of the grateful Samaritan leper, suggest Jesus' interest in people outside his own nation and foreshadow the universal mission. Luke's Gospel shows a peculiar social and humanitarian interest; the poor and unfortunate appear in it as the especial objects of Jesus' sympathy and help. A few echoes of medical language in the Gospel too remind us that Luke was, as Paul calls him in Colossians, "the beloved physician."[8]

SUGGESTIONS FOR STUDY

1. *References:* [1]I Cor. 11:23; [2]I Cor. 15:3–7; [3]Luke 1:1–4; [4]Luke 2:49; [5]Luke 4:16–21; [6]Luke 6:20–49; [7]Luke 10:1; [8]Col. 4:14.

2. Read Luke 1:1–4, noting what is implied as to previous narratives about Jesus.

3. Notice Luke's use of the first person in his preface, in contrast to the anonymity of Matthew and Mark.

4. Notice his historical purpose (cf. 1:5; 2:1, 2; 3:1, 2, 23), the sources he has, and how he means to use them.

5. Why did the existence of numerous accounts lead Luke to write another one?

6. Although Luke seems clearly to have used Mark, he omits one account of the feeding of the multitudes and the account of the cursing of the fig tree. Why does he do this?

7. Notice that, in addition to the infancy narrative (chaps. 1, 2), two considerable parts of Luke (6:20— 8:3; 9:51—18:14) contain no material found in Mark.

8. Notice the remarkable parables of Luke: the Lost Sheep, the Lost Coin, the Lost Son (chap. 15), the Pharisee and the Publican (18:9–14).

9. The passage from Isaiah which appears in Luke 4:18, 19 has been called the frontispiece of the Gospel of Luke. Why?

CHAPTER XI

THE ACTS OF THE APOSTLES

Within fifty years after the death of Jesus his gospel had spread over Palestine and Asia Minor and had been carried by travelers and missionaries across the Aegean Sea to Greece and over the Mediterranean to Rome. Companies of Christian believers had been formed in the principal cities, and the new faith was spreading rapidly. But few of these new Christians had any clear idea of how the gospel had reached their communities, and by what providential means and through what perils and difficulties the missionary travelers had found their way to Corinth, Ephesus, and Rome. Few had any idea of how the Christian movement had first separated itself from the Jewish faith; how it had ever come to be offered to Greeks, when it had originally belonged exclusively to Jews; where this change in the propagation of the gospel had begun, and who had first undertaken to carry the gospel out of Syria and Palestine into the other provinces of the Roman Empire.

Some men still lived who had seen this wonderful Greek mission develop and who had learned from others how it had begun. They knew what courage and perseverance and faith it had taken to bring

about its spread through the Roman world, and
they felt that it would strengthen the faith and
stimulate the zeal of the Christian believers around
them to hear the story from the beginning. In
such a spirit the physician Luke, perhaps in some
city on the Aegean Sea like Ephesus or Corinth,
began to write the story of the Greek mission.

He was himself a Greek, and knew little about
the beginnings of the movement except what others
had told him. But he was a close friend of Paul,
who had done more than any other to carry the
gospel among the Greeks of the Roman provinces.
He had been with Paul on some of his most dangerous and adventurous journeys and in some of his
most extraordinary experiences.[1] With him he had
visited Antioch, Caesarea, and Jerusalem, and
in these cities he had met people who could tell
him much about the strange series of events that
had led the earliest Christians to push out first
from Jerusalem to Caesarea and Antioch, and then
from Antioch to Cyprus and Galatia. Luke had
himself witnessed the extension of the movement
from Asia Minor to Macedonia and Achaea, and
had finally followed its progress to Rome itself.
Supplementing his experiences by his inquiries,
Luke fitted himself to relate the fascinating story,
with its bewildering variety of riots, arrests, trials,
councils, voyages, shipwrecks, imprisonments, and
escapes. These are set in the most varied scenes:

temples, market-places, deserts, islands, syna-
gogues, the courts of kings and governors, the
streets of those splendid flourishing cities of the
Greco-Roman world, Antioch, Ephesus, Corinth,
Athens, Rome. And over it all is the writer's conviction of the providential hand of God shaping
the decisions and movements of his people to his
own great purposes.

Luke felt this missionary movement to be so
natural a sequel to the ministry of Christ that he
made this work a companion volume to his life of
Christ.[2] In both of them his purpose is at once
religious and historical. He wishes to strengthen
the faith of his readers and commend Christianity
to them. At the same time he wishes to make their
knowledge of Christian history more exact and
complete. We should have liked more definiteness
in the dating of some events, and here and there
we long for a line more about the fate of Paul or
of Peter, the work of missionaries in the East and
South, or the beginning of Christianity in Alexandria or Rome. But we must admit that Luke has
told his story to its climax, for with the churches
once established in Antioch, Ephesus, Corinth, and
Rome, the extension of the gospel to the rest of
the Roman world about the Mediterranean was
inevitable.

We are now accustomed to view history as a
study of popular forces working their way to ex-

pression and influence, rather than of battles, reigns, and dynasties. With such a sense of historical values Luke wrote his sketch of the mission to the Gentiles. Kings and wars play little part in it. It is a record of a popular movement, at first obscure, then gradually making itself felt in widening circles and with increasing power. Even when he wrote, it was still little thought of and, indeed, hardly noticed by Greek or Roman historians and literary men. It was left for this Greek physician, the friend and fellow-traveler of Paul, to begin the writing of what we now call church history.

SUGGESTIONS FOR STUDY

1. *References:* [1]Acts 16:11; 27:1, 2; Col. 4:14; Philem. vs. 24; [2]Acts 1:1.

2. Compare the preface of Luke, 1:1–4, with the opening lines of Acts, 1:1, 2.

3. Notice that the conclusion of the Gospel (24:49–53) is reviewed in the following verses of Acts, 1:3–12, so that the narrative of Acts is closely joined to that of Luke.

4. Note that the descent of the Spirit in Acts 2:1–4 is in fulfilment of the promise recorded in Luke 24:49.

5. Notice the many lands from which Peter's hearers at Pentecost came, and to which those of them who were converted would return with the gospel.

6. Notice the constant emphasis of the Holy Spirit, the Spirit of God, and the Spirit of Jesus in Acts.

7. Read Acts 1–7 as an account of the development of the early church in Jerusalem.

8. In chaps. 8–12 note the gradual spread of the movement to proselytes and Gentiles in Samaria, Damascus, Joppa, Caesarea, and especially Antioch (11:20). Locate these places on the map.

9. Note that this instinctive, unorganized missionary movement at length takes definite shape at Antioch, 13:3.

10. Trace Paul's movements through Cyprus, Galatia (chaps. 13, 14), Macedonia, Achaea (chaps. 16–18), and Asia (chap. 19).

11. Observe that after Paul's arrest Luke continues to trace his movements and experiences until he has spent two years at Rome.

12. Consider why Luke should have stopped at this point. Did he write at this time? Or did he purpose to follow Paul's fortunes farther in a third book? Or had he reached his goal in tracing the establishment of churches through the gentile world from Judaea to Rome?

13. Notice those parts of Acts (16:10–18; 20:5–16; 21:1–18; 27:1–28:16) in which the writer speaks in the first person, the so-called "we sections." Consider whether there is any reason for thinking them to be by another hand than that which wrote the Acts. Where else does Luke speak in the first person?

14. Notice that Acts includes many accounts of wonders performed by apostles and others, not all of which are beneficent in character (5:1–11; 13:11).

CHAPTER XII

THE REVELATION OF JOHN

It was a dangerous thing in the first century to be a Christian. Jesus himself had laid down his life for his cause, and the apostles Paul, Peter, James, and John met their deaths as martyrs, that is, witnesses, to the new faith.[1] Yet to be a Christian was not against the Roman law, and through the first century we can trace the Christians' hope that when at length the Roman government should decide what its attitude toward Christians was to be, the decision would be favorable. Luke points out that Pilate himself was disposed to release Jesus, and expressly says that neither Herod nor Pilate found any fault in him.[2] Luke also brings out the fact that the proconsul Gallio at Corinth would not even entertain a charge against Paul, and that at Caesarea both Agrippa and the procurator Festus declared that Paul might have been released if he had not appealed to the emperor.[3] Paul had encouraged his converts to honor the king, that is, the emperor, and obey the law, and in Second Thessalonians had referred to the emperor as a great restraining power holding the forces of lawlessness in check.[4]

Nero's savage outbreak against the Roman church must have startled and appalled Christians all over the world, but that attack, though severe, was short, and left the status of Christians before the law undecided as before. Nero's victims suffered under the charge of burning the city, not that of being Christians, and Paul himself, as Luke indicates, was tried and probably executed as an agitator, not as a Christian. It is clear that representative Christians like Luke kept hoping that when a test case arose the Empire would not condemn the Christian movement and put Christians under its ban.

But these hopes were doomed to disappointment. Late in the reign of Domitian, the emperor-worship which had prevailed in some parts of the Empire since the time of Augustus began to threaten the peace of the churches. Earlier emperors had for the most part let it take its course, but Domitian found divine honors so congenial that he came to insist upon them. There was indeed an obvious political value in binding together the heterogeneous populations of the Empire, differing in speech, race, civilization, and religion, by one common religious loyalty to the august imperator, considered as in a certain sense divine. Most oriental peoples found this easy. Worshiping numerous gods, they did not much object to accepting one more.

With the Christians it was very different. Their faith forbade such an acknowledgment, and the scattered churches of Asia, where the matter first became acute, now witnessed the disappointment of their cherished hope of freedom to worship God undisturbed, in their own way. It is hard to realize all that this meant to them. Their early teachers had been mistaken. The Empire was not their friend and safeguard, to be loyally obeyed. It now suddenly appeared in its true colors as their bitter and unrelenting foe. For it inexorably demanded from them a worship of the emperor which Christians must refuse to accord. The church and the Empire were finally and hopelessly at war.

The Christian leaders of Asia must have realized this with stricken hearts, and they must have reviewed the history of the Christian movement from a new point of view. After all, what else could they have expected? Jesus, Paul, and Peter had suffered death for the Kingdom of God, and at the hands of Rome. In Nero's day hundreds of others had perished in Rome at the emperor's bidding. The Empire, as they now saw, had long since recorded its verdict, and it had been against them.

The matter of worshiping the emperor came home to the Christians of Asia in various forms. His name and likeness appeared on many of the coins they used. He had among them his provincial priesthood, charged with the maintenance of his worship throughout Asia. Christians might be called upon, as Pliny tells us they were twenty years later, to worship the image of the emperor. It was customary to attest legal documents—contracts, wills, leases, and the like—with an oath by the fortune of the emperor. Refusal to make this sworn indorsement would at once involve one in suspicion and lead to official inquiries as to the apparent disloyalty of the person concerned to the imperial government. Why not then make the oath? It was after all a purely formal matter with all who used it. Why not simply add to one's business documents, as everyone did, the harmless words, "And I make oath by the Emperor Domitianus Caesar Augustus Germanicus that I have made no false statement"? So slight an accommodation might seem a very excusable way to gain security and peace.

But in even slight concessions to pagan practice the Christian leaders of Asia saw a serious peril. There must be no compromise. The church might perish in the conflict, but the conflict could not be avoided. The church must brace itself for the struggle, and compromising was not the way to begin. On the contrary, the church must absolutely disavow everything pertaining to the wicked system through which the devil himself was now assailing it. For in the Empire the Asian Christians now recognized not a beneficent and protecting power but an instrument of Satan.

Among the first victims of the kindling persecution was a Christian prophet of Ephesus, named John. He seems to have been arrested on the charge of being a Christian and banished to the neighboring island of Patmos, perhaps condemned to hard labor. He could no longer perform for his Asian fellow-Christians the prophet's work of edification, comfort, and consolation described by Paul in First Corinthians,[5] though they needed it now as never before. But he might hope to reach them by letters, and, as he wrote these to the seven leading churches of Asia, his message expanded into a book. He uses the cryptic symbolic forms of the old Jewish apocalypses, of Daniel or Enoch, in which empires and movements figure in the guise of beasts and monsters, and the slow development of historical forces is pictured as vivid personal conflict between embodiments of rival powers. Indeed, his message is one that may not be put in plain words, for it contains a bitter attack upon the government under which the prophet and his readers live.

The canon of the writings of the prophets had long been regarded by the Jews as closed, and anyone who wished to put forth a religious message as a work of prophecy had therefore to assume the name of some ancient patriarch or prophet. But the Christians believed the prophetic spirit to have been given anew to them, and a Christian prophet had no need to disguise his identity. John in Patmos writes to the neighboring churches as their brother, who shares with them the agony of the rising persecution.

The task of the exiled prophet was to stiffen his brothers in Asia against the temptations of apostasy and compromise which the persecution would inevitably bring. He would arouse their faith. In the apparent hopelessness of their position, a few scattered bands of humble people arrayed against the giant world-wide strength of the Roman Empire, they needed to have shown to them the great eternal forces that were on their side and insured their final victory. For in this conflict Rome was not to triumph, but to perish.

The prophet's letters to the seven churches convey to them the particular lessons that he knows they need. But one note is common to all the letters. "To him that overcometh," to the victor in the impending trial, the prophet promises a divine reward. But this is only the beginning of his message. Caught up in his meditation into the very presence of God, the prophet in the spirit sees him, as Isaiah saw him, enthroned in ineffable splendor.[6] In his hand is a roll crowded with writing and sealed seven times to shut its contents from sight. Only the Lamb of God

proves able to unfasten these seals and unlock the
mysterious book of destiny, which seems to contain the will of God for the future of the world, and
to need to be opened in order to be realized.
Dreadful plagues of invasion, war, famine, pesti-
lence, and convulsion attend the breaking of the
successive seals, doubtless reflecting familiar contemporary events in which the prophet sees the
beginning of the end. On the opening of the
seventh seal seven angels with trumpets stand
forth and blow, each blast heralding some new
disaster for mankind. Despite these warnings
men continue in idolatry and wickedness. The
seventh trumpet at length sounds and proclaims
the triumph of the Kingdom of God, to which the
prophet believes all the miseries and catastrophes of
his time are leading.

The victory is thus assured, but it has yet to
be won. The prophet now sees the dragon Satan
engaged by the archangel Michael and the heavenly
armies. Defeated in heaven, the dragon next as-
sails the saints upon the earth. In this campaign
Satan has two allies, one from the sea—the Roman
Empire—the other from the earth—the emperor
Domitian, or the priesthood of his cult. Again
the prophet's vision changes. Seven bowls symbolizing the wrath of God, now at last irrepressible,
are poured out upon the earth. An angel shows
him the supreme abomination, Rome, sitting on

seven hills and drunk with the blood of the saints. Another angel declares to him her doom, over which kings and merchants lament, while a thunderous chorus of praise to the Lord God Omnipotent arises from the redeemed. The prophet's thought hastens on from the fate of persecuting Rome and the imprisonment of Satan to the glorification of those who have suffered martyrdom rather than worship the emperor. As priests of God they reign with Christ a thousand years, until the great white throne appears, and the dead, small and great, stand before it for the final judgment.

These lurid scenes of plague and convulsion now give way to the serene beauty of the new heavens and the new earth, with the new Jerusalem coming down out of heaven from God who makes all things new. Amid its glories God's servants, triumphant after their trial and anguish, serve him and look upon his face.

The prophet begins with a blessing upon anyone who shall read his prophecy and upon those who shall hear it read. He closes with a warning against any tampering with its contents. The book is clearly intended to be read at Christian meetings. More than this, by its repeated claim of prophetic character, it stands apart as the one book in the New Testament that unequivocally declares itself to be Scripture. It is thus in a real sense the nucleus of the New Testament collection.

The Revelation is not a loyal book. Its writer hates the Roman government and denounces its wickedness in persecuting the church in unmeasured terms which every Christian of the day must have understood. It does not indeed advise rebellion, but it is, from an official Roman point of view, a seditious and incendiary pamphlet. But so symbolic and enigmatical is its language that few outside of Jewish or Christian circles can have understood its meaning, or guessed that by Babylon the prophet meant the Roman Empire. Its value to the frightened and wavering Christians of Asia must have been great, for it promised them an early and complete deliverance, and cheered them to steadfastness and devotion. Their trial indeed proved less severe than they had feared, for twenty years later Ignatius found these same churches strong and earnest, and forty years after the writing of Revelation a Christian convert named Justin found this book still prized by the Ephesian church. Ignatius and Justin both suffered martyrdom in Rome, and joined the army of those who had come out of great tribulation, and had made their robes white in the blood of the Lamb. But in these successive conflicts, and through many more down to the present day, Christians have cheered themselves in persecution with the glowing promises and high-souled courage of the banished prophet of Ephesus, who in the face of hopeless defeat and destruction showed a faith that looked through death, and in stirring and immortal pictures assured his troubled brethren of the certain and glorious triumph of the Kingdom of God.

SUGGESTIONS FOR STUDY

1. *References:* [1]Mark 10:35, 39; Acts 12:2; John 21:18, 19; [2]Luke 23:14–16; [3]Acts 26:31, 32; [4]II Thess. 2:7; [5]I Cor. 14:3; [6]Rev., chap. 4.

2. Read Dan., chaps. 7, 8, as examples of Jewish apocalyptic.

3. Read Rev., chaps. 1–3, noticing the light they throw upon the state of Christianity in Asia.

4. Read chap. 4, the prophet's vision of God, noting its resemblance to Isa., chap. 6, and Ezek., chap. 1.

5. Notice in chaps. 6–11 the seven seals leading up to the seven trumpets, each one symbolizing some invazion, earthquake, slaughter, disaster, or other of the Last Woes.

6. Notice in chaps. 12, 13 the war against the church begun in heaven and continued on earth by the dragon and his allies.

7. Observe in chaps. 15, 16 the seven bowls of wrath preluding the destruction, in chaps. 17, 18, of Rome, the persecutor of the church.

8. Notice that chap. 20 presents the climax of the whole in the judgment scene, while chaps. 21, 22 describe the city of God and the happiness of his people, now delivered from their persecutors.

9. Observe the solemn warning of the prophet against any tampering with his work, 22:18, 19.

10. What are the main religious ideas underlying all this oriental imagery?

CHAPTER XIII

THE EPISTLE TO THE HEBREWS

Of all the early centers of Christianity the church at Rome went through the most significant and dramatic experiences. Founded by unknown persons about the middle of the first century, it entertained Paul and Peter, Luke and Mark, witnessed the martyrdom of the chief apostles and piously tended their graves, in a single generation withstood the fires of two persecutions, and served in short as the focus of Christian life in the capital of the world.

All this was not effected without sacrifice and devotion. It is the Christians of Rome who first appear in the pages of the history of the Empire, and it was the extraordinary sufferings they endured that led the historian to mention them.[1] Hardly a dozen years after the Roman church had been established there burst upon it the storm of Nero's persecution, of brief duration but of frightful severity. Many of the Christians of Rome suffered agonizing martyrdom, and all of them faced it with a heroism that wrung sympathy even from the callous populace of that brutal city. In that dreadful August of 64 A.D. the Roman Christians learned what it was to have their dearest friends

and leaders torn from them, to attend these friends
to prison and to cruel and mocking deaths, to lose
their little savings by capricious confiscation, and
so to be brought by the events of a single month to
the very verge of ruin and despair.

From such a baptism of fire the Roman Christians emerged reduced in property and numbers,
but more than ever convinced that they were pil-
grims upon the earth and that their citizenship
was in heaven. They were sustained in this by the
hope in which Paul and Peter had confirmed them,
that Jesus would soon return to set up his messianic
kingdom, and that then their troubles would be
over. Their immediate troubles did soon pass and
gave way to a reasonable degree of security and
peace, but the hope of Jesus' coming remained
unfulfilled.

Years went by. The churches settled down
from their first exuberant spiritual enthusiasm into
a partial accommodation to a work-a-day world.
They had their officers, their meetings, their insti-
tutions. They still expected the return of Jesus,
but only as people might who had been expecting
it all their lives. The expectation could hardly
play the part in their religious lives that it had in
their fathers'. But evidences were beginning to
appear that they were in turn to be put to the test
to which Nero had put their predecessors. Domitian was emperor. Conspiracies and losses had

embittered and frightened him. He had begun in Rome that reign of terror which so horrified high-minded Romans like Tacitus who had to witness it.

What first led Domitian to threaten the Roman church is not clear. It may have been his insist-ence upon divine honors for himself, as it was in Asia. It may have been the collection for the benefit of Jupiter Capitolinus, of the temple tax from the Jews, and the incidental confusing of Christians with the latter. Or perhaps the in-ability of a Christian magistrate to perform the religious duties his office imposed upon him first brought the Christians again under attack. At any rate, toward the very end of Domitian's life, he made a series of attacks upon the Christians of Rome which left a deep impression upon them.

The Roman church had more than made up the losses Nero had inflicted upon it. It had continued to practice that duty of Christian hospitality which its location imposed upon it, and to attend to the needs of Christian prisoners who were brought to Rome as Paul had been. It had not, however, developed any outstanding Christian teachers, nor as yet taken the place of leadership among the churches for which its position at Rome naturally marked it out. It was a practical church, but a church without imagination. The fact that Jesus had been executed like a slave or a criminal was hard for it to understand and to harmonize with the messiahship he claimed. And with the passing of time the expectation of Jesus' return to the earth had declined in eagerness and confidence, leaving the Roman Christians far less ready to withstand the shock of persecution than their fathers had been thirty years before.

. But persecution and apostasy were not the only dangers that threatened the Roman church. The very age of the church now exposed it to a peril of apathy and indifference which could never have menaced it in its youth, when enthusiasm was new and hope high. While some might continue to hold in a mild way their expectation of Jesus' coming, others, now that the generation that had known Jesus in Galilee had passed away and Jesus had not returned, felt that the expectation so long disappointed had been vain, and that the Christian movement was played out.

It was to this situation that some Christian teacher, unknown to us but well known at Rome, addressed the letter which from its strongly Jewish tone has come to be called the Epistle to the Hebrews. The writer was not in Italy, though other Christians from Italy were with him when he wrote, and perhaps from what they had told him, or from what he had himself observed in Rome, the perilous situation of the Roman community was clear to him. But the Roman church must not go down. Its noble traditions of devotion and service must not sink into oblivion. Above all the great task for which it was in the writer's mind so clearly marked out must be performed. The church must not only survive but rise to higher forms of service, that should eclipse all that it had yet done. This is the kindling ideal that this great unknown of the first century puts before the wavering line of Roman Christians. Seeing them unequal to their present task, he nerves them for a greater.

The Christian scholar who undertook to meet this situation took as his theme the complete and final character of the revelation made in Christ. As compared with the beings, men or angels, through whom the old Jewish revelation was made, Christ is immeasurably superior. They were at best God's servants; he is God's son. How shall anyone escape who neglects a salvation so supremely authoritative? The Romans must learn the awful lesson of the Israelites in the wilderness. Like them they have had good news and set forth for a better country; let them not like the Israelites, through unbelief and disobedience, fall short of the heavenly rest.

Christ is not only far above the old mediums of revelation; he is far superior to the old priests. This is a difficult matter to explain to the Romans, who for all their long experience as Christians, in view of which they ought to be teaching and leading the churches, are still no better than infants as far as intellectual or spiritual development is concerned. Only let them remember that persons who have once had the Christian experience and who then give it up can never recover it. It is impossible to renew them again unto repentance. Surely none of the Christians at Rome will make this irreparable mistake. Their faithful service of helpfulness to their needy brethren has long commended them to God; they must not give up now, but hold fast to the end.

To show his readers the extraordinary value of what they are in danger of throwing away, the writer proceeds to explain to them the messianic priesthood of Christ and its superiority to the old Jewish priesthood. In doing this he uses the Old Testament in the fanciful Alexandrian manner, treating it allegorically and typically. This enables him to find in the Old Testament evidence that Jesus is the final and eternal high priest, of an order older than Aaron and even than Abraham. His ministry is correspondingly superior to that of the Jewish priests. They had to offer over and over again, in a tent that was at best only a copy of the heavenly sanctuary, the same material and ineffectual sacrifices. But Christ as messianic high priest has offered once for all in the heavenly sanctuary the supreme sacrifice of himself and taken his seat at the right hand of God.

With this novel and ingenious interpretation of Jesus' religious significance the writer couples the practical lesson of drawing near to God through the new and living way which Jesus has opened. He again exhorts the Romans to keep fast hold of their Christian hope. He who has promised is faithful; already they can see the Day drawing near. To return to a life of sin after having once experienced the Christian salvation is to forfeit that salvation forever and to incur penalties too dreadful to utter. It is a fearful thing to fall into the hands of the living God. They must remember the heroic devotion they showed in former days, when in its infancy their church endured a cruel persecution at Nero's hands.[2] That same boldness and endurance they must still show.

Through all the history of God's dealings with men, that faculty of faith by which men have laid firm hold on the unseen realities has kept patriarchs, prophets, and martyrs steadfast to the end. These veterans of faith are now looking down upon their successors at Rome to see them run with endurance the race upon which they have started. Christ himself has set the supreme example of faith. In all the trials and hardships that they are enduring the Romans must learn to see God's paternal discipline, by which the lives and characters of his sons are to be perfected.

In a final impassioned utterance the writer returns to the thought with which he began. The new covenant and mediator are far above their old Jewish prototypes, and disloyalty to them is attended with proportionately greater peril. Our God is a consuming fire.

Exhortations and warnings conclude the letter. The Romans must not forget the noble example of their first martyr-teachers. Considering the issue of their lives, they must imitate their faith. They must avoid false teachings and practices, and be thankful and beneficent. The writer closes his hortatory discourse, as he calls it,[3] with the news of Timothy's release from prison, promises to visit them soon, and sends salutations from himself and the Italian brethren who are with him.

The language of Hebrews shows more elegance and finish than that of any other book of the New Testament. Its author was a trained student and thinker. What he wrote is so eloquent as to be more like an oration than a letter, and the absence of any superscription such as letters usually have makes it seem all the more oratorical. It is worth noting that the Judaism which the writer has in mind is always that of the tabernacle in the wilderness, never that of the temple in Jerusalem. In showing the superiority of Christ's covenant and revelation, he first among Christian writers makes free use of that allegorical interpretation of the

Old Testament which has had such grave conse-
quences in Christian history. Hebrews may be
regarded as the supreme effort of early Christianity
to state the religious significance of Jesus in Jewish
terms—"mediator," "high priest," "Messiah." It
is interesting to observe that the Roman church
bravely withstood the attack of Domitian and in
the century that followed made an earnest effort
to teach and lead its sister churches in a way
worthy of its opportunities and its history.

SUGGESTIONS FOR STUDY

1. *References:* [1]Tacitus, *Annals* xv. 44; [2]Heb. 10:32–35;
[3]Heb. 13:22.

2. Consider Heb. 10:32–34 as a picture of the experiences of the Roman Christians during Nero's persecution.
Compare with it Tacitus' account, especially these sentences:
"First those were seized who confessed that they were
Christians. Next on their information a vast multitude
were convicted, not so much on the charge of burning the
city, as of hating the human race. And in their deaths
they were also made the subjects of sport, for they were
covered with the hides of wild beasts and worried to death
by dogs or nailed to crosses or set fire to and when day
declined burned to serve for nocturnal lights. Nero offered
his own gardens for the spectacle."—Tacitus, *Annals* xv. 44
(translation in Harper's Classical Library).

3. Note the stately, often rhetorical, language of Hebrews, for example, 1:1–4; chap. 11; 12:1, 2.

4. Note that Hebrews calls itself a hortatory discourse,
"the word of exhortation," 13:22. Can it be a Christian
sermon afterward sent to another congregation as a letter?

5. In this case would the personal references and appeals appropriate to one circle be appropriate also to the other?

6. Notice the successive comparisons of Christ with (1) the angels, who were in Jewish thought the mediums of revelation, chaps. 1, 2; (2) with Moses, 3:1–6; (3) with Joshua, 4:8–11; (4) with Aaron, 7:11–28.

7. Read 8:1—10:39, observing the argument that Christ performs a priestly service of a higher type than that of the Jewish priests.

8. Read chaps. 11, 12, noting the writer's idea of faith as the faculty of laying hold on the unseen, and his argument that his readers should, like the heroes of faith, find in their trials the discipline of their faith.

9. Notice the frequent paragraphs of practical exhortation: 2:1–4; 3:12–14; 4:1, 2, 11, 14–16; 6:11, 12.

10. What is the writer's view of those who have given up their faith in Christ and apostatized? Cf. 6:4–6; 10:26–31.

11. Who were the martyr-teachers of the Roman church whose example the writer commends to the Romans in 13:7?

12. Notice the rebuke of ascetic practices in the commendation of marriage, 13:4, and the reference to meats, 13:9.

13. Notice the continued use of somewhat extended letters in the life of the early church. Had Paul's example something to do with this?

CHAPTER XIV

THE FIRST EPISTLE OF PETER

The Empire's condemnation put a peculiar strain upon the churches all over the Roman world. The ignorant masses already regarded the Christians as depraved and vicious and credited them with eating human flesh and with other monstrous practices. But quite aside from this the Empire had adjudged being a Christian a crime punishable by death. The Christian had neither the protection of the state nor the sympathy of his fellows.

In this situation a Christian elder of Rome wrote to his brethren throughout Asia Minor a letter of advice and encouragement. Perhaps the Epistle to the Hebrews had already reached Rome and its ringing challenge to the Romans to be teachers stirred him to write.[1] He styles himself a witness of Christ's sufferings, which may mean that he was himself a Christian confessor, that is, one who had risked his life by acknowledging his faith before the authorities.[2] He sends to the Christians of the chief provinces of Asia Minor a message of hope. They already enjoy a salvation of unutterable worth, and have awaiting them in heaven an imperishable inheritance. All their present trials are to prove and refine their faith. As Christians they are to live lives of holiness and love. By their pure and unobjectionable conduct they must disarm the public suspicion of their practices. They must obey the emperor and his appointed governors. Government is for the restraint of evildoers and for the encouragement of the good. The example of Christ's sufferings should encourage servants when they are mistreated to imitate his patience and self-command. All must cultivate sympathy, humility, and love.

No one can reasonably molest them if they live uprightly, but if they should suffer for their very righteousness they would be only the more blessed. It is better to suffer for welldoing than for evildoing. They must not be afraid, but be ready to give respectful and honest answers to magistrates who examine them, and by their uprightness of life must silence and condemn the popular calumnies. Christ too suffered to bring them to God, and they must live the new Christian life which he opened to them, not their old gross heathen life of sin.

The fiery trial to which they are now exposed must not be thought strange. Through it they may share in Christ's sufferings, and so in his coming glory too. It is a privilege to endure reproach for the name of Christ. To be punished for committing crime carries disgrace along with it, but to endure punishment for being a Christian

does honor to God. They can only commit their
lives to God, and keep on doing what is right.

Their elders must do their work in a noble and
high-minded way, as true shepherds of the flock of
God under the chief shepherd Christ. They must
all humble themselves under God's mighty hand,
and he will in his good time lift them up again.
Everywhere their Christian brethren are being
compelled to endure this same bitter experience.
God is the source of all their help, and after they
have suffered a little while he will give them deliverance.

Among the messages which conclude the letter
is one from the church at Rome—here as in the
Revelation called Babylon—in which the writer
is an elder.[3] Who he was it is not possible to say;
but in later times, when the name of Peter was
being connected with the Roman church, he naturally came to be considered the author of the first
great Christian letter, after Paul, that had gone out
from Rome. Hebrews and First John do not name
their writers, but the titles given these books in most
Bibles ascribe them to definite authors, and something like this probably happened to First Peter.
But, whoever wrote it, it gave the imperiled Christians all through Asia Minor a message of hope and
courage during the persecution of Domitian, pointed
out the difference between suffering for being a
criminal and suffering for being a Christian, and

inspired them to overcome by lives of purity and goodness the hatred and slanders of the heathen world.

1. *References:* [1]Heb. 5:12; [2]I Pet. 5:1; [3]Rev. 17:5, 6, 9.

2. Read First Peter through, and imagine its effect upon the persecuted Christians of Asia Minor.

3. Notice the districts of Asia Minor in which Christianity was already established, 1:1. Consider whether the order in which they are mentioned is that in which the bearer of the letter would naturally visit them.

4. Which of these had Paul evangelized?

5. In view of the hostile attitude of the Empire, how do you explain the loyal tone of the letter, 2:13–17?

6. How does this compare with the attitude of the writer of the Revelation, in the same general circumstances?

7. What does the writer imply in speaking of Rome as Babylon, 5:13?

8. Notice the help for the situation of his readers found by the writer in the suffering of Christ, 3:18; 4:1.

9. Observe the emphasis upon suffering "as a Christian," 4:15, 16. Was this a new thing? The victims of Nero's persecution had suffered under the charge of being incendiaries or haters of the human race.

10. What picture of church life and of Christian morals does the letter give?

11. Note that four ancient documents relate to Domitian's persecution in Rome and Asia Minor: Revelation, Hebrews, First Clement, and First Peter.

12. Observe the strange idea that Christ had preached to the dead, which first appears in I Pet. 3:18–20; 4:6.

13. On Christianity in Bithynia (1:1) read Pliny's letter to Trajan (x.97) written about 112 A.D., a few years

after First Peter. Pliny inquires of the emperor "whether the very profession of Christianity unattended with any criminal act, or only the crimes themselves attaching to the profession are punishable. . . . . An anonymous information was laid before me containing a charge against several persons who upon examination denied that they were Christians or had ever been so. They repeated after me an invocation to the gods and offered religious rites with wine and incense before your image, which for that purpose I had ordered to be brought, together with those of the gods, and even reviled the name of Christ, whereas there is, it is said, no forcing those who are really Christians into any of these compliances. I thought it proper therefore to discharge them." Some who had been Christians "affirmed that the whole of their guilt or their error had been that they met on a stated day before it was light and addressed a form of prayer to Christ as to a divinity, binding themselves by a solemn oath not for the purposes of any wicked design, but never to commit any fraud, theft, or adultery, never to falsify their word nor to deny a trust when they should be called upon to deliver it up; after which it was their custom to separate and then reassemble to eat in common a harmless meal. From this custom, however, they desisted after the publication of my edict by which according to your commands I forbade the meeting of any assemblies. After receiving this account I judged it so much the more necessary to extort the real truth by putting to the torture two female slaves who were said to officiate in their religious rites, but all I could discover was evidence of an absurd and extravagant superstition. . . . ."—Pliny, *Letters* x. 97 (Bosanquet's translation in Bohn's Classical Library).

CHAPTER XV

THE EPISTLE OF JAMES

The ancient world was full of preachers. Dressed
in a rough cloak, one would take his stand at some
street corner and amuse and instruct, with his easy,
animated talk, the chance crowd that gathered
about him. He would mingle question and answer,
apostrophe, dialogue, invective, and anecdote,
urging his little congregation to fortitude and self-
control, the great ideals of the Stoic teachers. For
these street preachers of ancient times were Stoics,
and their sermons were called diatribes.

Christian preachers had to compete with these
men for the attention of the people they were trying
to convert to Christianity, and they naturally
adopted some of their methods. In the market-
place at Athens Paul did this informal open-air
preaching every day, and in doing so came into
conflict with some of these Stoic preachers.[1] A
later Stoic, Justin, became a Christian, and tells
us in his *Dialogue with Trypho* how he continued
to practice this way of preaching on the promenade
at Ephesus.

We cannot help wishing that one of these street
sermons had been preserved to us just as its author
gave it, and of course we have in the Book of Acts
reports of several sermons of Stephen, Peter, and

Paul. It is true that Luke was not present when most of these were uttered, and probably had to fill out somewhat any outline or report which had come to him; but this only means that the sermon, if not exactly what Paul or Peter said, is what another early Christian preacher, Luke, would have said, or supposes Paul would have said, in those circumstances. But we have in the New Testament at least one ancient sermon preserved for its own sake and not as an incidental part of a historical narrative. It is the book we know as the Epistle of James.

In James the Christian preacher tells his hearers that life's trials, vicissitudes, and temptations will perfect character, if they are met in dependence upon God. But his hearers must not merely profess religion, but really practice purity and humanity. They must be doers that work, not hearers that forget. They must learn to respect the poor, and to feed and clothe the needy. Their faith must show itself in works. They must not be too eager to teach and direct one another. The tongue is the hardest thing in the world to tame. If they wish to show their wisdom, let them do it by a life of good works. They must give up their greed, indulgence, and worldliness, their censoriousness and self-confidence. Their rich oppressors are doomed to punishment; only they must be patient, like Job and the prophets. Above all

things, they must refrain from oaths. In trouble
and sickness they must pray for one another. The
prayer of a righteous man avails much. And they
must seek to convert sinners, for God especially
blesses such work.

These are the teachings of this ancient sermon.
What is the connection between them? Do they
constitute a chain of thought? Are they beads
on a string, or simply a handful of pearls? As an
example of Christian preaching this sermon is not
at all doctrinal or intellectual. Little is said even
of Christ. The whole emphasis is practical. The
preacher's interest is in conduct, in the words and
acts of his hearers. He does not care especially
about their theological views. For him the only
real faith is that which shows itself in good deeds.
Honest, upright, and helpful living is what the
preacher demands, and he does so with a directness
and a frankness never since surpassed. It is this
that has given this fifteen-minute sermon its abiding place in Christian literature.

Where this sermon was first preached it is impossible to say. It would have been appropriate
almost anywhere. That is the beauty of it. But
we may be sure that it was as a sermon and not as a
letter that it first appeared. It contains none of
those unmistakable epistolary touches that we find
for example in Galatians and Second and Third
John. It does not end with a farewell or benedic-

tion as so many New Testament letters do. Only
the salutation contained in the first verse suggests a
letter: "James, a servant of God and of the Lord
Jesus Christ, to the twelve tribes which are of the
Dispersion, greeting."

But a moment's reflection will show that this
does not prove the Epistle of James to be a letter.
How would one go about delivering it "to the
twelve tribes which are of the Dispersion," that is,
to the Jews scattered about through the Greco-
Roman world from Babylon to Spain? Or, if the
Dispersion is meant in a figurative sense, to all
the Christians outside of Palestine? It is clear at
once that these words are not the salutation of a
letter but a kind of dedication for a published work.
That the Epistle of James was written to be thus
published, however, that is, that it is an "epistle"
in the literary sense of the word, is very improbable
in view of its contents, which relate to no single
subject or situation.

It can surely be no cause for surprise or incredu-
lity that we possess among the twenty-seven books
of the New Testament one representative of the
commonest type of Christian literature, the sermon. It would be a wonder if this were not the
case. Like thousands of other sermons, it was not
only preached but published, with a dedication,
boldly figurative, to Christians everywhere. The
unidentified James whose name is prefixed to it

may have been its author or its publisher, or simply one in whose name it was put forth. The
early church sought to recognize in him Jesus'
brother, who, though not an apostle, became the
head of the church at Jerusalem;[2] but if he was
the preacher, the sermon's reticence about Jesus
would be doubly hard to understand.

There is something very modern about this so-
called Epistle of James. Its interest in democracy,
philanthropy, and social justice strikes a responsive
chord in our time. The preacher's simplicity and
directness, his impatience with cant and sham and
his satirical skill in exposing them, his noble advo-
cacy of the rights of labor and his clear perception
of the sterling Christian virtues that were to win
the world, justify the place of honor his sermon
has in the New Testament.

SUGGESTIONS FOR STUDY

1. *References:* [1]Acts 17:17, 18; [2]Gal. 1:19; 2:12.

2. Is the teaching of James as to faith and works incom-
patible with Paul's teaching as to faith, or only different
from it in emphasis?

3. What did Paul mean by "works," and what does the
letter of James mean?

4. Are the rich oppressors of 5:1–6 worldly Christians,
or is the passage an apostrophe in which the preacher con-
demns the luxury and heartlessness of the pagan world?
Cf. 2:6, 7.

5. What evils does the letter principally attack?

6. What are its chief religious teachings?

7. Do the practical teachings of the letter resemble those of Jesus as we know them from the Gospels, and if so, which ones?

8. Read it through aloud at a single reading, and imagine its effect upon a first-century company of Christians in some house in Rome or Corinth.

9. Do you observe in James any traces of the preacher's acquaintance with First Peter?

10. Compare James with typical prophetic sermons, Amos, chaps. 1, 2; Isa., chap. 1 or chap. 5 or 8:1—10:4 or chaps. 18, 19, the sermon on Egypt.

11. Compare with James a discourse of Epictetus: for example, i, 3, i, 16, or the following: "Have you not God? Do you seek any other while you have him? Or will he tell you any other than these things? If you were a statue of Phidias, either Zeus or Athena, you would remember both yourself and the artist, and if you had any sense you would endeavor to do nothing unworthy of him who formed you or of yourself, nor to appear in an unbecoming manner to spectators. And are you now careless how you appear because you are the workmanship of Zeus? And yet what comparison is there either between the artists or the things they have formed? . . . . Being then the formation of such an artist, will you dishonor him, especially when he has not only formed but intrusted and given to you the guardianship of yourself? Will you not only be forgetful of this but moreover dishonor the trust? If God had committed some orphan to your charge, would you have been thus careless of him? He has delivered yourself to your care, and says, 'I had no one fitter to be trusted than you. Preserve this person for me such as he is by nature; modest, faithful, sublime, unterrified, dispassionate, tranquil.' And will you not preserve him?"—Epictetus, *Discourses* ii. 8 (Carter's translation).

CHAPTER XVI

THE LETTERS OF JOHN

About the beginning of the second century a disagreement arose among the Christians of Asia. It was about the reality of the life and death of Jesus. How could the Messiah, the Son of God, possessed of a divine nature so utterly removed from matter, have lived a life of human limitation and suffered a shameful and agonizing death?

It was a favorite idea in ancient thought that the material universe was intrinsically evil, or at least opposed to goodness, and that God, being wholly good, could not come into any direct contact with it, for such contact, it was thought, would infect God with the evil inherent in all matter. This idea was held by some Christians who at the same time accepted Jesus as the divine Messiah. From this contradiction they escaped in part by claiming that Jesus' divine nature or messiahship descended on him at his baptism and left him just before his death on the cross. They inferred that his sufferings were only seeming and not real, and from this idea they were known as Docetists, that is, "seemists."

The Docetists were probably better educated to begin with than most Christians, and their profession of these semi-philosophical views of Christ's life and death still further separated them from ordinary people. This separation was increased by the claim they made of higher enlightenment, closer mystic fellowship with God, clearer knowledge of truth, and freedom from sin. Expressions like "I have fellowship with God," "I know him," "I have no sin," "I am in the light," were often on their lips. Both their spiritual pretensions and their fantastic view of Christ made them an unwholesome influence in the Asian churches and roused more than one Christian writer to dispute their claims.

There lived at that time in Asia a Christian leader of such influence and reputation that he could in his correspondence style himself simply "the Elder." Wide as his influence must have been, there were some who withstood his authority and refused to further his enterprises. With his approval missionaries had gone out through Asia to extend the gospel among the Greek population. Some Christians had welcomed them hospitably and helped them on their way, but others who were hostile to the Elder had refused to receive them and had threatened any who did so with exclusion from the church.

In this situation the Elder writes two letters. One, known to us as Third John, is to a certain Gaius, to acknowledge his support and encourage

him to continue it, and to warn him against the
party of Diotrephes. Gaius is probably the most
influential of the Elder's friends and supporters in
his own community, while Diotrephes is the leader
of the party hostile to the Elder. The letter
is probably delivered by Demetrius, one of the
missionaries in question. At the same time the
Elder writes another short letter, our Second John,
to the church to which Gaius belongs, urging its
members to love one another and to live harmoniously together, and warning them against the
deceivers who teach that Christ has not come in
the flesh. The advocates of this teaching they are
to let severely alone, refusing them even the ordinary salutations and the hospitality usual among
Christians. The two letters are brief, for the
Elder is coming to them very soon in person; but
short as they are they bring us into the very heart
of a controversy that was already dividing individual churches and threatening the peace of a
whole district.

As missionaries like Demetrius went about the
province of Asia, under the Elder's direction, they
took with them a longer letter from his pen in
which the same pressing matters were more fully
presented. We have seen that the short letters
are without his name, and the long letter bears
not even his title. It hardly required it if it was
to be carried by his messengers and read by them

as from him in the assembled churches they visited. This longer letter, known to us as First John, deals with the same question as Second John, takes the same view of the matter, and puts it with the same confident authority. But the situation has developed somewhat, for the Docetists, or some of them, have now left the church.[1]

The Elder begins with the most confident emphasis. His own experience guarantees the truth of his message, which he is sending in order that his readers may share the fellowship with God and Christ which he enjoys.[2] The heart of that message is that God was historically manifested in the life of Christ, and that the Christian experience is fully sufficient for anyone's spiritual needs. To claim fellowship with God and live an evil life will not do; the claim is false. The Docetic pretension to sinlessness is mere deceit. The Christian way is to own one's sins and seek forgiveness.

The claim of knowing Christ is meaningless apart from obedience to his commands. Living as he lived is the only evidence of union with him. Those who claim peculiar illumination and yet treat their brethren with exclusiveness and contempt show that they have never risen to a really Christian attitude. The Elder's reason for writing to his friends is that they have laid the foundation of a real Christian experience, and he would warn them against sinking again into a life of worldliness and sin.

The breach with the Docetic thinkers, with their claims of freedom from sin, is complete. It is well that they have left the church, for they have no right to be in it. Those who deny that Jesus is the Christ are not Christians but antichrists. In opposition to their teachings, true Christians should continue to cultivate that spiritual experience upon which they have entered. They must abide in Christ and following the guidance of the Spirit seek, as children of a righteous heavenly father, to be righteous like him. Righteousness and love are the marks of the Christian life. Jesus in laying down his life for us has shown what love may be.

Some who urge the Docetic teaching claim that the Holy Spirit in their hearts has indorsed it. But the Spirit of God authorizes no such teaching. Only spirits that confess that Jesus Christ is come in the flesh are of God. Spirits that deny this are of the world. The Elder declares that he is of God, and that all who really know God will obey his solemn warning against these spirits of antichrist.[3]

Love is the perfect bond in all this great spiritual fellowship. Love is of God and God is love. He has shown it by sending his Son into the world to give us life. We love because he first loved us. If he so loved us, we also ought to love one another. Belief in Jesus as the Christ is the sign of sonship

to God and the way to the life of love, since it
is the manifestation in Jesus of God's love that
kindles love in us.   The messiahship of Jesus is evi-
denced not only by the voice of the Spirit, but by
his human life and death.   There are three who
bear witness, the Spirit, and the water, and the
blood.   The witness is this, that God has given us
eternal life and this life is in his Son.   To have the
life we must see in Jesus the Christ, the indispen-
sable revelation of God.

The Elder writes to confirm his readers in their
assurance of eternal life.   Sonship to God means
the renunciation of sin.   The Christian has an
inward assurance that he belongs to God, whom
Jesus has revealed.   Here is the true God and
eternal life.

Except for a few touches which mark it very
definitely as a letter (2:12–14), this little work
might pass for a sermon or homily.   It is clearly a
circular letter written to save the churches of Asia
from the Docetic views which threatened them.
The great words of the letter, life, light, love, figure
importantly in the Fourth Gospel also, and in its
meditative and yet epigrammatic style the letter
resembles the Gospel.   It has been said that
while the Gospel argues that Jesus is the
Christ, the letter contends that the Christ is Jesus,
that is, the Messiah is identical with the historical
Jesus.

Who was this Asian Elder who could so confidently instruct and command the churches of his countryside? Early Christian writers mention an Elder John of Ephesus, who had been a personal follower of Jesus but was not the apostle of that name, and they sometimes refer to him simply as "the Elder," just as the writer of these letters calls himself. There is no need to identify him with the prophet John of the Revelation. But to John the letters have always been ascribed, and we may think of the Elder John as sending them out from Ephesus, one to Gaius, one to the church to which he belonged, and one to that and other churches, in full assurance that the Christian experience and belief in Jesus as the Christ would save them from the mistakes of Docetism.

SUGGESTIONS FOR STUDY

1. *References:* [1]I John 2:19; [2]I John 1:1–4; [3]I John 4:6.

2. Read Third John as an example of a personal Christian letter. Compare it with Paul's letter to Philemon, the only other one of this kind preserved in the New Testament.

3. Read Second John as an example of a letter to a church, analogous with Paul's letters to Thessalonica, Corinth, or Colossae. How does it compare with such letters of Paul?

4. Notice in First John the emphasis on belief in Christ, 2:23; 3:23; 4:15; 5:10–13. How does this compare with the teaching of James? Yet cf. 3:18.

5. Notice the writer's attitude to the world as over against the church, 2:15–17; 3:13; 5:19. Is there anything like this in James?

6. Read First John, noting the spiritual claims made by the Docetists but denied by the writer, 1:6, 8, 10; 2:4, 9; 4:20.

7. Has the reference to antichrists in 2:18 anything to do with what Paul wrote of in Second Thessalonians, or is it merely an application of the well-known name to the new and immediate foes of the church?

8. Does the "going out" of the Elder's opponents from the church, 2:19, mark the beginning of the rise of heretical bodies professing a modified Christianity not accepted by the church at large? Consider whether the Nicolaitans of Rev. 2:6, 15 may have been such a Christian sect.

9. What are the leading religious ideas of First John?

10. Read 4:7-21, comparing it with Paul's chapter on love, I Cor., chap. 13.

11. The letter begins with basing Christian confidence on Christian experience, 1:1-4. What is its closing emphasis, 5:18-21?

CHAPTER XVII

THE GOSPEL ACCORDING TO JOHN

Christianity and Judaism had parted company. The Christian movement, at first wholly Jewish, had after a little tolerated a few Greeks, then admitted them in numbers, and at length found itself almost wholly Greek. The Jewish wing of the church withered and disappeared. The Jews closed up their ranks and disowned the church. Church and synagogue were at war.

It was plain that the future of the Christian movement lay among the Greeks, the Gentiles. To them it must more than ever address itself. Its message must be made intelligible to them. But the forms in which it had always been put were Jewish. Jesus was the Messiah, the national deliverer whose coming was foretold by Jewish prophets, and who was destined to come again on the clouds of heaven in fulfilment of the messianic drama of Jewish apocalyptic. The church was addressing a Greek world in a Jewish vocabulary. Was there no universal language it could speak? Was no one able to translate the gospel into universal terms? The Gospel of John is the answer to this demand.

Early in the second century a Christian leader of Ephesus, well acquainted with the early Gospels

and deeply influenced by the letters of Paul, put
forth a new interpretation of the spiritual significance of Jesus in terms of Greek thought.   Paul
had laid great emphasis upon faith in Jesus the
risen Christ, glorified at God's right hand, and had
attached little importance to knowing the historical
Jesus in Palestine.   His Ephesian follower finds in
Paul's glorified Christ the divine "Word" of Stoic
philosophy, and reads this lofty theological conception back into the earthly life of Jesus. The
faith Paul demanded becomes with him primarily
an intellectual assent to the messiahship of Jesus
thus understood, that is, to the revelation in the
historical Jesus of that absolute divine will and
wisdom toward which Greek philosophy had always
been striving.

The form in which this Christian theologian put
his teaching was a gospel narrative. He did not
intend it to supersede the familiar narratives of
Matthew and Luke, but to correct, interpret, and
supplement them. The new narrative differs from
the older ones in many details. In it Jesus' ministry
falls almost wholly in Judaea instead of Galilee, and
seems to cover three years instead of one. The
cleansing of the temple is placed at the beginning
instead of at the end of his work. Nothing is
said of Jesus' baptism, temptation, or agony in
the garden. His human qualities disappear, and
he moves through the successive scenes of the

Gospel, perfect master of every situation, until at the end he goes of his own accord to his crucifixion and death. He does not teach in parables, and his teaching deals not, as in the earlier Gospels, with the Kingdom of God, but with his own nature and with his inward relation to God. In his debates with the Jews he defends his union with the Father, his pre-existence, and his sinlessness. He welcomes the interest shown by Greeks in his message, prays for the unity of the future church, and interprets the Lord's Supper even before he has established it. His cures and wonders, which in the earlier Gospels seem primarily the expression of his overflowing spirit of sympathy and helpfulness, now become signs or proofs to support his high claims.

The long delay of the return of Jesus to the world had caused that hope which had been so strong at first to decline in confidence and power. The new evangelist at once acknowledges and explains this by showing that the return of Jesus has already taken place in the coming of his spirit into the hearts of Christian believers. He thus transforms the Jewish apocalyptic expectation into a spiritual experience.[1] He foresees that under the guidance of this spirit the Christian consciousness will constantly grow into greater knowledge and power.

Toward the close of his Gospel the writer states his purpose in writing it to be to give his readers

faith in Jesus as the Christ, and thus to enable
them to have life through his name.[2] This idea of
the life to be derived from Jesus is prominent in the
whole Gospel. Christ is the source of life of a real
and lasting kind, and it can only be obtained
through mystic contact with him. This is because
Jesus is the full revelation of God in human life.
This doctrine, which we call the Incarnation, is
fundamental in the Gospel of John: "In the beginning was the Word and the Word was with God
and the Word was God. . . . . And the Word became flesh and dwelt among us, and we beheld his
glory. . . . . I am come that they may have life and
that they may have it abundantly."

While the Gospel of John contains no parables,
in a sense it is a parable. It presents an interpretation of Jesus in the form of a narrative of his
ministry. The writer feels that the Jewish title of
Messiah does not express the full religious significance of Jesus, but by finding for it an expression
in Greek philosophical terms he transplants Christian thought and the Christian movement into
Greek soil. It was easy for persons of Greek
education to understand the claim that Jesus was
the divine Logos, or Word, of the Stoic philoso-
phers, and a gospel which began with such a claim
would be likely to arrest their attention. The
writer still thinks of Jesus as Messiah, and retains
his respect for the Jewish scriptures. Indeed, the

idea of the revealing Word of Jehovah appears now and again in Jewish literature, and the Jewish philosopher Philo had already identified it with the Logos of Greek thought. This made it all the easier for the writer of the new Gospel to apply it to Jesus, but in this interpretation of Jesus as the divine Word he goes beyond previous Christian thinkers and takes a long and bold step in the development of Christian theology.

The Gospel is the story of Jesus' gradual revelation of himself to his disciples and followers. The opening sentences present its main ideas in words intelligible and attractive to Greek minds. Over against the followers of John the Baptist, who still constituted a sect in the writer's day as they had in Paul's,[3] the evangelist relates John's ready testimony to Jesus as the Son of God and Lamb of God. With a few followers, some of them directed to him by John, Jesus visits Cana and in the first of his "signs" indicates his power to transform human nature.[4] After a brief stay in Capernaum he goes to Jerusalem to the Passover, and there clears the temple of the dealers in sacrificial birds and animals who with their traffic victimized the people and disturbed places meant for prayer. The Jews demand a sign in proof of his right to do this, and he answers with a prophecy of his resurrection. In a conversation with Nicodemus, Jesus explains that a new birth of water and the Spirit, that is, baptism and spiritual illumination, must precede the new life of the Kingdom. Jesus comes near the place where John is baptizing and John gives fresh testimony to his superiority. To avoid overshadowing John, Jesus goes into Galilee,[5] and on the way explains the water of life to a Samaritan woman and reveals himself as the Messiah and the source of eternal life. In Galilee Jesus is favorably received and performs the second of the seven signs that punctuate his earthly ministry. Soon another feast brings him to Jerusalem. There he heals an impotent man on the Sabbath and, in the discussions which ensue with the Jews, expounds his relation to God. Returning to Galilee, he feeds a great multitude by the Sea of Galilee and declares himself the bread of life, for everyone who beholds him and believes on him shall have eternal life. At the Feast of Tabernacles he is again in Jerusalem, teaching in the temple, although danger from the Jewish authorities threatens him. He declares that he is sent by God and offers his hearers the water of life, which the evangelist interprets to mean his Spirit, which was to be given to his followers after his resurrection. He proclaims himself the light of the world and when the Jews object claims the witness of God for his message. He promises truth and freedom to those who abide in his words, and declares his sinlessness and pre-existence. He restores a blind man's sight on the

Sabbath, and in the discussions that follow declares himself the Son of God and the Good Shepherd. Soon after at Bethany Jesus raises Lazarus from the dead and proclaims himself the Resurrection and the Life. The hostility of the Jewish rulers becomes so bitter that he conceals himself for a little while in Ephraim, but as the Passover approaches he goes up to Bethany. Enthusiastic crowds go out from Jerusalem to meet him and escort him in messianic state into the city. Greeks ask that they may meet him, and Jesus answers that he is now to be glorified but that it must be through his death. In his last hours with his disciples he comforts them in preparation for his departure, and promises to send them his spirit to comfort and instruct them. Under the figure of the vine and the branches he teaches them the necessity of abiding in him, the source of life. As he has come from the Father so now he must return to him. Finally, in an intercessory prayer, he asks God's protection for his disciples and the church they are to found.

Leaving the city, he goes with his disciples to a garden on the Mount of Olives. There Judas brings a band to arrest him, but they are at first overawed by his dignity, and only after securing the freedom of his disciples does Jesus go with them.[6] He is examined before the high priests and before Pilate, and on the charge that he claims to

be the king of the Jews he is sentenced to be crucified. The evangelist is careful to show that Jesus
retains his sense of divine commission to the last
and dies with the words, "It is finished," on his
lips, and he bears solemn testimony to the piercing
of his side and the undoubted reality of his death.
These details were important for the correction of
the Docetic idea that the divine spirit abandoned
Jesus on the cross. The writer also indicates that
Jesus was crucified on the day before the Passover,
so that his sacrificial death fell on the day on which
the Passover lamb was sacrificed. On this point he
corrects the earlier gospel narratives.

Early on the first day of the following week
Jesus appears to Mary. The same evening he
appears to the disciples, imparts his spirit to them,
and commissions them to forgive sins. Eight days
later he again appears to them when Thomas is
with them and convinces Thomas of the reality of
his resurrection. The Gospel closes with the evangelist's statement of his purpose in writing it: that
his readers may believe that Jesus is the Christ,
the Son of God, and that, believing, they may have
life in his name.

To the Gospel of John an appendix or epilogue
was afterward added.[7] It reports an appearance
of the risen Jesus by the Sea of Tiberias, or Galilee,
and his conversation on that occasion with Peter,
in which he predicts Peter's death, but seems to

intimate that the beloved disciple may live until his own return. The Gospel never names this disciple, but by describing him several times in this way it makes him more conspicuous than any name could make him. The beloved disciple has perhaps died, for the epilogue explains that Jesus did not exactly say that the beloved disciple would survive until his coming. This epilogue may have been added to the Gospel to correct the popular misunderstanding about Jesus' words to Peter, and to claim the beloved disciple's authority and even authorship for the Gospel. There are indeed some points in the Gospel which seem to involve better information on the part of its writer than the earlier evangelists had. But the whole character of the narrative and its evident preference for the symbolic and theological, as compared with the merely historical, are against the assigning of its composition to a personal follower of Jesus. It is very probable that it was written by that Elder of Ephesus who perhaps after the publication of this Gospel wrote the three letters that bear the name of John.

The Gospel of John was wholly successful in what it undertook. It was not at first generally welcomed by the churches, but in the course of half a century it came to be accepted side by side with the earlier Gospels, and in its influence upon Christian thought it finally altogether surpassed them.

Its great ideas of revelation, life, love, truth, and freedom, its doctrine of the spirit as ever guiding the Christian consciousness into larger vision and achievement, and its insistence upon Jesus as the supreme revelation of God and the source of spiritual life, have given it unique and permanent religious worth.

SUGGESTIONS FOR STUDY

1. *References:* [1]John 14:3, 16–18, 23, 26, 28; 15:26; [2]John 20:31; [3]Acts 19:1–7; [4]John 2:11; [5]John 4:1, 2; [6]John 18:8, 9; [7]John, chap. 21.

2. Read John 1:1–18, noting in the passage the leading ideas of the whole Gospel: revelation, incarnation, and Christ the source of life and light.

3. Notice in 2:13–16 that the cleansing of the temple is put early in Jesus' ministry. Where in his work do our other Gospels put it?

4. Count Jesus' visits to Jerusalem in John and the number of Passover feasts mentioned in the course of Jesus' ministry, 2:13; 5:1; 6:4; 7:2, 10; 10:22, 23; 12:1, 12.

5. How long a ministry does this imply? How many passovers and visits to Jerusalem does Mark record?

6. Note the seven signs wrought by Jesus before his crucifixion, 2:11; 4:54; 5:9; 6:11; 6:19; 9:7; 11:43, 44. Cf. 20:30.

7. Why does the evangelist record these signs and how does he interpret them? Cf. 20:31.

8. Are the discourses in John mainly ethical, like the Sermon on the Mount; eschatological, like Mark, chap. 13; theological; or apologetic, that is, in defense of the pre-existence, messiahship, or authority of Jesus?

9. With all its emphasis upon belief (20:31), note the other, mystical, side of the Gospel's teaching, 15:1–19. Do you see any resemblance here to First John?

10. Notice that the writer speaks frequently of "the Jews" as over against Jesus and his followers, though these latter were Jews too in the period of Jesus' ministry. Consider whether this suggests that he wrote at a time when the Christians and the Jews were sharply distinguished.

11. Someone has said that there are a hundred quotations from Matthew, Mark, and Luke in the Gospel of John. Can you find any such?

12. Mark 14:12–17 puts the Last Supper on the day on which the Passover lamb was sacrificed. Are John 13:1; 18:28; 19:14, meant to correct this?

13. Is the writer's conception of Christ more like Paul's or Mark's?

14. Is his idea of Jesus' return to the earth like Paul's?

15. What is the religious value of the Gospel of John?

CHAPTER XVIII

THE LETTERS TO TIMOTHY AND TO TITUS

The first Christians were too absorbed in the expectation of Jesus' speedy return to the earth to give much thought to practical detail. They cared nothing about developing a literature, a theology, or an organization. The Lord was at hand.[1] The time was short.[2] Why should people marry or slaves seek to be freed? At any moment the present order might come to an end.

But time wore on and nothing happened. The first leaders passed away, but the churches continued their work. It began to be clear that the end was not to come as speedily as men had thought, and that the churches might have to go on under the existing order for a long time. Christian leaders began to see that the practical side of church life could no longer be neglected. Spiritual enthusiasm and well-meaning devotion were no longer enough. Efficiency must be insured. Church life must be regulated. Church officers must be properly qualified. The several classes of people in the churches must be shown their several spheres and functions and kept to them. Efficiency must come through organization.

Such a state of things, it is true, seems a serious decline from the high, confident, spiritual enthusiasm of the apostolic age. But after the prophet must come the priest, to conserve and codify the other's work. And this was what the letters to Timothy and to Titus sought to do.

Many churches needed to be shown what officers they ought to have to carry on their work and what kind of men these ought to be. Marriage, it was now evident, ought to be encouraged and sanctioned. The charitable work of the churches must be wisely directed and protected from abuse. The morals of the Christian communities needed definite correction. Christian leaders needed to be reminded that they must set a worthy example of conduct and character. The homely practical lessons which need to be taught so often had to be put before the widest possible circle of churches in compact and telling form.

In these letters Christians are taught to pray for kings and rulers and for all men. Perhaps the empire has not yet shown its hostile attitude to the church. Yet First Peter, written in the midst of persecution, bids Christians honor the emperor.[3] Certainly the Book of Revelation takes a very different attitude toward kings. Prayer is to be offered by men. Women are not to teach, but to occupy a subordinate place in the church life. Each church may have as officers a presiding officer, the bishop or elder, and his assistants, the deacons. These should be men of good repute and blameless character, who have married but once. A recent convert should not be made a bishop, and only men who have proved their faithfulness in the church life should be appointed deacons.

That practical helpfulness which had characterized the churches from the first finds natural expression in providing for the support of destitute widows in the Christian community. This matter needs to be safeguarded against abuse. It is right that children or grandchildren who are able to do so should provide for their widowed mothers or grandmothers. Only widows past middle life and without any kindred able to provide for them are to become the permanent pensioners of the church.

Novel religious speculations remote from practical life are to be discouraged and avoided. Some teachers have declared that the resurrection has already taken place; an idea perhaps due to a misunderstanding of Paul's teaching that conversion and baptism usher the believer, risen with Christ, into a new and blessed life. Such innovations are to be sternly condemned.

It was the coming in of these new currents of teaching that most perplexed Christian leaders toward the end of the first century. How were they to be met and controlled? They sometimes seemed to threaten the life of the churches. To whom, when the first great leaders of Paul's generation were gone, could their less gifted successors appeal in matters of conscience and faith? This is one of the questions these epistles to Christian ministers undertake to answer. It is not easy to realize how far early Christian thought, on a great many matters, was from being definite and specific. The words of Jesus all recognized as authoritative, and also the voice of his Spirit in their own hearts. But one Christian might put forth views widely different from another's and claim for them the authority of the Spirit. Which was right? Who was to decide?

In the midst of this rising confusion of belief and teaching the churches fell back upon the letters of Paul. New teachings that conflicted with his must be false. In addition to Paul's letters and the memory of his teaching there was also what we call the Old Testament. Jesus had disowned various parts of it, and Paul had denied the religious efficacy of the Law, but Christian leaders felt safer in following them in their indorsement of the Jewish scriptures than in their partial rejection of them, and very definitely added the Old Testament to their new authorities. We have evidence of this tendency in the Gospels of Matthew and John, but it is Second Timothy that first puts it decisively and unequivocally. Every scripture inspired of God, it was now felt, was profitable for teaching, reproof, and instruction. The church had adopted the Old Testament.[4]

With the words of Jesus, a few letters of Paul, and the Jewish scriptures at their backs, the Christians could now feel in a measure prepared to test new religious teachings which original spirits in their own community or Christian visitors from distant churches might set forth in the local meetings. The new teaching had to square with the old apostolic teaching. If it conflicted with that, it could not stand. It must be possible also to harmonize it with the Old Testament. That Paul and Jesus did not always conform to the Old Testament did not at once appear nor greatly matter. What was needed was authorities, and with Jesus, Paul, and the literature of the Old Testament the need was satisfied.

That the letters to Timothy and Titus claim Paul as their author may be due to the fact that short genuine letters of his were made the basis of them by some later follower of Paul who composed them. At any rate, the writer felt justified in claiming Paul's authority for what he thought a necessary and timely supplement to the letters Paul had left behind, and doubtless thought he was doing just what Paul would have done had he lived to see the conditions the writer saw. But the value of these letters lay in the practical direction they gave the churches of their time, showing them how

to readjust their high hopes of Jesus' return and
to set themselves to the task of establishing and
perpetuating their work. In these little letters we
see the church after the lofty enthusiasm of its
first great experience settling down to the common
life of the common day and grappling with its age-
long task.

SUGGESTIONS FOR STUDY

1. *References:* [1]Phil. 4:5; [2]I Cor. 7:29; [3]I Pet. 2:17;
[4]II Tim. 3:16.

2. Notice that First Timothy is a letter of instruction
to a Christian pastor or minister, 4:6, and that his public
functions are reading, exhortation, and teaching, 4:13.
What would he read in church? Cf. II Tim. 3:15, 16.

3. Read I Tim. 3:1-13, noticing the church officers
mentioned and the qualifications they ought to have. What
is the chief emphasis in these?

4. Note the writer's somewhat indiscriminate condemnation of the advocates of a different type of Christian
teaching, I Tim. 4:1-3; II Tim. 3:1-9; Titus 1:10-16.
Does he give a clear picture of their teachings?

5. Notice the writer's indorsement of marriage, I Tim.
3:2, 12; 4:1-3; Titus 1:6.

6. Observe the writer's rule as to women teachers, I
Tim. 2:11, 12. Cf. Acts 18:26.

7. What is meant in these letters by "faith"? Is it an
inward attitude of trust and dependence upon God or a
deposit of truth to be guarded and preserved?

8. In what does the Christian life consist, according to
these letters?

9. Do any of Paul's great characteristic ideas appear in
these letters?

10. Is II Tim. 4:6–8, which we may call Paul's epitaph, any less appropriate or significant, considered as an early Christian's estimate of Paul, than when viewed as Paul's own commendation of himself?

11. What would be the immediate practical value of these letters to the scattered pastors and ministers of the early churches?

CHAPTER XIX

THE EPISTLE OF JUDE AND THE SECOND EPISTLE OF PETER

Many ancient thinkers conceived of the supreme God as far removed from the material world and too pure to have anything directly to do with it. The necessary connection between God and the world, they thought, was made through a series of intermediate ideas, influences, or beings, to one of which they ascribed the creation and supervision of the material world. When people with these views became Christians, they brought most of their philosophical ideas with them into the church and combined them as far as they could with their new Christian faith.

In this way there came to be many Christians who held that the God of this world could not be the supreme God whom Jesus called his Father. Their view of Jesus himself seemed to most Christians a denial of him, for they held to the Docetic idea that the divine Spirit left him before his death. They accordingly saw little religious meaning in his death, but they considered themselves so spiritual that they did not feel the need of an atonement. In fact, they felt so secure in their spirituality that they thought it did not much matter what they did in the flesh, and so they permitted themselves without scruple all sorts of indulgence.

Such people could not help being a scandal in the churches, and a Christian teacher named Jude made them the object of a letter of unsparing condemnation. He had been on the point of writing for some Christian friends of his a discourse on their common salvation when word reached him that such persons had appeared among them. He immediately sent his friends a short vehement letter condemning the immoral practices of these people, predicting their destruction, and warning his readers against their influence. He quotes against them with the greatest confidence passages from the Book of Enoch[1] and the Assumption of Moses,[2] late Jewish writings which he seems to regard as scripture. The persons he attacks still belong to Christian churches and attend Christian meetings. He does not tell his readers to exclude them from their fellowship but to have pity on them and to try to save them, only taking care not to become infected with their faults.

Who this Jude was we cannot tell. He looks back upon the age of the apostles, asking his readers to recollect how they have foretold that as time draws on toward the end scoffers will appear. He probably wrote early in the second century. The words "the brother of James" were probably added to his name by some later copier of his letter who took the writer to be the Judas or Jude mentioned in Mark 6:3 and Matt. 13:55 as a brother of James and Jesus.

A generation after this vigorous letter was written it was taken over almost word for word into what we know as Second Peter. In the early part of the second century various books were written in Christian circles about the apostle Peter, or even in his name, until one could have collected a whole New Testament bearing his name. There were a Gospel of Peter, Acts of Peter, the Teaching of Peter, the Preaching of Peter, the Epistles of Peter, and the Revelation of Peter. Most of these laid claim to being from the pen of Peter himself.

The one that most insistently claims Peter as its author is our Second Peter. It comes out of a time when Christians were seriously doubting the second coming of Jesus. A hundred years perhaps had passed since Jesus' ministry, and men were saying, "Where is his promised coming? For from the day the fathers fell asleep all things continue as they were from the beginning of creation." The spiritualizing of the second coming which the Gospel of John wrought out did not commend itself to the writer of Second Peter, if he was acquainted with it. He prefers to meet the skepticism of his day about the second coming with a sturdy insistence on the old doctrine. In support of it he appeals to the Transfiguration, which he seems to know

from the Gospel of Matthew,[3] and to the wide-
spread ancient belief that the universe is to be
destroyed by fire.[4] He repeats the denunciation
which Jude hurled at the gnostic libertines of his
day, only it is now directed against those who are
giving up the expectation of the second coming.
Jude has some hope of correcting and saving the
persons he condemned, but the writer of Second
Peter has no hope about those whom he attacks.
He supports his exhortations by an appeal to the
letters of Paul.[5] He evidently knows a number of
them, for he speaks of "all his letters." He con-
siders them scripture, and says that many misin-
terpret them, to their own spiritual ruin. This
view of the letters of Paul, combined with the use
in Second Peter of other New Testament books,
proves it to be the latest book in the New Testament. It was not addressed to any one church or
district, but was published as a tract or pamphlet,
to correct the growing disbelief in the second
coming of Jesus; and to enforce his message its
writer put it forth, as other men of his time were
putting forth theirs, under the great name of Peter.

SUGGESTIONS FOR STUDY

1. *References:* [1] Jude, vss. 14, 15; [2] Jude, vs. 9; [3] II Pet.
1:16–18; [4] II Pet. 3:10; [5] II Pet. 3:15, 16.

2. Note the picture drawn in Jude of the errorists under
discussion, vss. 4, 8, 10, 12, 16, 18, 19, and the writer's
unsparing denunciation of them.

3. Compare Jude, vss. 4–18, with II Pet. 2:1—3:3, noting the close resemblance.

4. Notice the quotations from late Jewish writings: from the Assumption of Moses in Jude, vs. 9, and from the Book of Enoch in Jude, vss. 14, 15. Does the writer regard these books as scripture?

5. Notice the vagueness of the address of Jude. To whom is it addressed or dedicated?

6. Doe Second Peter seem from its salutation, 1:1, to have been sent as a letter or published as a tract or pamphlet?

7. Notice in Second Peter the references to Jesus' prediction of Peter's death, 1:14 (cf. John 21:18, 19); to the Transfiguration, 1:17, 18, most resembling Matt. 17:5; to I Pet. (3:1), and to the letters of Paul, 3:15, 16.

8. What do these last verses imply as to the collection of Paul's letters, the esteem in which they were held, and the sectarian use being made of them in some quarters at the time when Second Peter was written?

9. Observe in II Pet. 3:3, 4 the writer's condemnation of those who have given up the expectation of the return of Jesus.

10. Notice the support the writer finds for his views in the Stoic doctrine that the material universe would ultimately be destroyed by fire, 3:10.

11. Compare the first clause of 3:10 with one in the earliest book in the New Testament, I Thess. 5:2. Is this a quotation—the writer of Second Peter knows some letters of Paul (cf. 3:15)—or a coincidence?

CHAPTER XX

THE MAKING OF THE NEW TESTAMENT

When the latest book of the New Testament had been written, there was still no New Testament. Its books had to be collected and credited with a peculiar authority before the New Testament could be said to exist. What led to this collection and estimate?

For the first Christians the chief authority was Jesus. What he had taught they accepted as true and binding. Believing that his spirit still spoke in their own hearts, they ascribed the same authority to its inward directions.[1] Men who possessed this spirit in an especial measure, the Christian prophets, sometimes wrote down their revelations, and these came naturally to have the authority of scripture, that is, the authority which the Christian believers attached to the writings of the Old Testament. Jesus' teaching was at first handed down in the form of tradition; new converts learned it from those who were already Christians, and in turn taught it by word of mouth to those who became believers later.[2] But when gospels were written these began to take the place of this oral handing down, or tradition, of Jesus' words, and soon the gospel writing, and not simply the sayings of Jesus that it contained, came to be regarded as the authority. Authority thus gradually and naturally passed from the words of Jesus, and the thoughts of believers endowed with his spirit, to books embodying these.

Almost from the beginning, too, Christians had held Jesus' apostles in high esteem. Jesus had committed the continuation of his work to them. Paul, though not one of the Twelve, had by his zeal, devotion, and missionary success, convinced the churches that he too was in a real sense an apostle. His martyrdom gave added weight to the teachings he had left behind in his letters, and these came to be considered as Christian authorities of equal rank with gospels and revelations. Through the informal interchange of copies these books spread from church to church and came gradually to be read in the various churches in their meetings, along with the books of the Old Testament.

In the early years of the second century gifted but erratic Christian teachers began to divide the scattered and unorganized churches into parties or sects. Other Christian teachers, fearful of these schismatic tendencies, opposed these novel views and insisted upon what they considered the true and original Christian belief. In these controversies with heretics, that is, sectarians or schismatics, Christians in general more and more appealed in support of their views to the books and letters which had come down to them from earlier times and which they believed presented Christianity in its true and abiding form. In this way greater emphasis came to be laid upon the letters of Paul, the Gospels, and the Revelation.

The first step toward collecting early Christian writings of which we have any definite knowledge was taken strangely enough by one of these sectarian leaders, a certain Marcion, of Pontus in Asia Minor. He was a well-to-do ship-owner of Sinope. He had become convinced that the God of the Old Testament could not be identified with the loving heavenly Father whom Jesus proclaimed, and so he rejected the Old Testament. Something had of course to be put in its place for purposes of Christian worship and devotion, and Marcion proposed a Christian collection, consisting of the Gospel of Luke and ten letters of Paul. He did not include in this list the letters to Timothy and Titus. He accompanied his list with a work of his own called the Antitheses, in which he sought to show that the God of the Jewish scriptures could not be the God revealed in Jesus. The wide influence of Marcion must have done much to promote the circulation of the letters of Paul, whose interpretation of Christianity he regarded with especial favor.

About the same time Christian teachers in Asia put forth the Four Gospels together, perhaps in order to increase the influence of the Gospel of John, which Christians attached to the lifelong use of Matthew or Luke might find easier of acceptance if it were circulated along with the Gospel to which they were accustomed. But it is not until about 185 A. D. that we find anything like our New Testament in use among Christians. By that time a great effort had been made by leading Christians of the non-sectarian type—who regarded their form of teaching as apostolic—to unite the individual churches of East and West into one great body, to resist the encroachments of the sects. The basis of this union was the acceptance of a brief form of the Apostles' Creed, episcopal organization, and a body of Christian scriptures, substantially equivalent to our New Testament. In this way the Catholic, that is, the general or universal, church began.

The New Testament, as it soon came to be called, did not displace the Jewish scriptures in the esteem of the church, as Marcion had meant his collection to do. It stood beside the Old Testament, but a little above it, for the Old Testament had now to be interpreted in the light of the New. The books included in the New Testament were appealed to in debate with schismatics as trustworthy records of apostolic belief and practice. They served an even more important purpose in being read from week to week, in the public meetings of the churches, along with the Old Testament scriptures. The Jewish idea that every part of the Old Testament must have an edifying meaning was definitely accepted by early Christians, and was now applied by them to the New Testament as well. This obliged them, as it had the Jews, to interpret their sacred books allegorically, and so the historical meaning of the New Testament books was neglected and obscured, and finally actually forgotten.

As to what should be included in this library of preferred and authoritative Christian writings, there was agreement among the churches in regard to general outlines, but no little diversity of views as to details. All accepted the Four Gospels so familiar to us, and thirteen letters of Paul, including those to Timothy and Titus. The Acts of the Apostles and three or four epistles, one of Peter, one or two of John, and that of Jude, were also generally accepted. Eastern churches, especially that at Alexandria, holding Hebrews to be the work of Paul, put it into their New Testament, but it was nearly two hundred years before Rome and the western churches admitted this. The West, on the other hand, accepted the Revelation of John as early as the middle of the second century, but the East never fully recognized its right to a place in the New Testament. The lesser epistles of John, Peter, and James were variously treated, some accepting them and others refusing to do so.

The Syrian church never accepted them all, but in Alexandria and in the West they became at length established as parts of the New Testament, mainly on the strength of their supposed apostolic authorship.

Other books now almost forgotten found places in the New Testament in the third and fourth centuries. One of the oldest Greek manuscripts of the New Testament includes the so-called letters of Clement of Rome, one a letter from the Roman church to that at Corinth, written about the end of the first century, the other a sermon sent seventy years later from Rome to Corinth. Another of these manuscripts contains the Shepherd, a revelation written by a Roman prophet named Hermas, toward the middle of the second century, to bring the Roman church and other Christians to genuine and lasting repentance. The so-called Epistle of Barnabas, a curious work of a slightly earlier time, is also included in this old manuscript. These oldest extant copies of the New Testament were made in the fourth and fifth centuries, probably for church use, and show what books were considered scripture in those times in the places where these manuscripts were written.

The list of New Testament books that we know, that is, just the twenty-seven we find in our New Testament today, and no others, first appears in a letter written by Athanasius of Alexandria at Eas-

ter in 367 A.D. But long after that time there
continued to be some disagreement in different
places and among different Christian teachers as
to just what books were entitled to be considered
the inspired and authoritative Christian writings.
This was somewhat less felt than it would be now,
because the books of the New Testament were not
often all included in a single manuscript. People
would have one manuscript containing the Gospels,
another containing Paul's letters, a third containing the Acts and the general epistles—James, Peter,
John, Jude—and perhaps a fourth, containing the
Revelation. It was only when printing was in-
vented that the whole New Testament began to
be generally circulated in one volume, in Latin,
Greek, German, or English.

The value of the New Testament to the Christian church has of course been immeasurably great.
To begin with, the formation of the collection insured the preservation and the lasting influence
upon Christian character of the best of the earliest
works of Christian instruction and devotion. While
the purpose of the makers of the New Testament
was not historical, they nevertheless did a great
service for Christian history. But the idea of establishing a list of Christian writings which should
be exclusively authoritative, put fetters upon the
free Christian spirit which could not always remain. Indeed, the New Testament itself included

in Galatians the strongest possible assertion of that freedom, and so carried within itself the corrective of the construction which Catholic Christianity put upon it. But though Christians in increasing numbers may no longer attach to it the dogmatic values of the past, they will never cease to prize it for its inspiring and purifying power, and for its simple and moving story of the ministry of Jesus. Historically understood, the New Testament will still kindle in us the spirit which animated the men who wrote it, who aspired to be not the lords of our faith but the helpers of our joy.

SUGGESTIONS FOR STUDY

1. *References:* [1]I Cor. 7:40; 14:37; [2]I Cor. 11:2, 23; 15:3.

2. How did Paul, Mark, and Luke regard the sayings of Jesus? Cf. I Cor. 11:24, 25; Acts 20:35.

3. Did Paul believe that he had the authority of the Holy Spirit for some of his teachings? Cf. I Cor. 7:40; 14:37.

4. Did he think himself alone in this? Cf. 2:16; 7:40.

5. What did Paul think of an external written standard for the inner life? Cf. II Cor. 3:6.

6. Did the earliest Christians find their religious authority without, in books or laws, or within, in their spiritual intuitions?

7. Did the writer of the Gospel of Matthew think Mark too perfect to be freely revised?

8. Did Luke regard his sources, including Mark, as inspired or infallible? Cf. Luke 1:1-4.

9. How does the writer of Second Peter regard Paul's letters? Cf. 3:15, 16.

10. Note the classing of prophets and apostles together in Eph. 2:20; 3:5, and in Rev. 18:20.

11. Read Rev. 21:14, noting the high esteem in which a Christian prophet holds the apostles.

12. Note the full acknowledgment of the Jewish scriptures as inspired in II Tim. 3:16, 17.

13. What book of the New Testament claims to be inspired?

BIBLIOGRAPHY

GENERAL

MOFFATT, JAMES. *An Introduction to the Literature of the New Testament.* New York: Scribner, 1911.

The most complete and valuable introduction to the whole literature.

STREETER, B. H. *The Four Gospels: A Study in Origins.* New York: Macmillan, 1925.

BURTON, E. D. *Short Introduction to the Gospels.* Chicago: The University of Chicago Press, 1904.

A presentation of the main facts about the purpose and attitude of each Gospel necessary for reading it intelligently.

WREDE, W. *The Origin of the New Testament.* New York: Harper, 1909.

Four popular lectures on the origin of the books of the New Testament and of the New Testament itself, by a very able German scholar.

SODEN, H. VON. *The History of Early Christian Literature: The Writings of the New Testament.* New York: Putnam, 1906.

A fuller treatment along the same lines.

PEAKE, A. S. *A Critical Introduction to the New Testament.* New York: Scribner, 1911.

Good, compact introductions to the several books, with especial reference to recent opinion and discussion, which are clearly summarized and criticized.

BACON, B. W. *Introduction to the New Testament.* New York: Macmillan, 1900.

BACON, B. W. *The Making of the New Testament.* New York: Henry Holt, 1912.

These books cover the literature of the New Testament, the first book by book, the second in a more popular and continuous historical way.

McGIFFERT, A. C. *The Apostolic Age.* New York: Scribner, 1910.

Chaps. iv–vi deal fully and helpfully with the books of the New Testament in their relation to the history of early Christianity and the development of Christian thought.

Encyclopaedia Britannica, 11th ed., 1912.

Valuable articles on the several books.

HASTINGS, *Dictionary of the Bible.* New York: Scribner, 1909. 1 vol.

Good short articles on the several books.

SPECIAL

BACON, B. W. *Galatians.* (The Bible for Home and School.) New York: Macmillan, 1909.

A short popular commentary with a good introduction and an analysis of the letter.

MASSIE, JOHN. *Corinthians.* (New) Century Bible. New York: Frowde, 1902.

A good short commentary for popular use.

GILBERT, G. H. *Acts.* (The Bible for Home and School.) New York: Macmillan, 1908.

An excellent short commentary for the general reader.

HARNACK, A. *The Acts of the Apostles.* New York: Putnam, 1909.

The introduction to this volume will serve admirably to put the reader into the atmosphere of the Acts.

PORTER, F. C. *Messages of the Apocalyptic Writers.* New York: Scribner, 1905.

A popular treatment of the Revelation showing its historical situation and its relations with kindred Jewish literature.

GOODSPEED, E. J. *Hebrews.* (The Bible for Home and School.) New York: Macmillan, 1908.

A concise commentary for popular use, with a somewhat full introduction on the occasion, purpose, and date of the letter.

SCOTT, E. F. *The Historical and Religious Value of the Fourth Gospel.* (Modern Religious Problems.) Boston: Houghton Mifflin Co., 1909.

An admirable sketch, for the general reader, of the purpose, ideas, and worth of the Gospel of John.

LAKE, KIRSOPP. *The Earlier Epistles of St. Paul.* Second Edition. London: Rivingtons, 1914.

BURTON, E. D., and GOODSPEED, E. J. *A Harmony of the Synoptic Gospels for Historical and Critical Study.* New York: Scribner, 1917.

CASE, SHIRLEY J. *The Revelation of John: A Historical Interpretation.* Chicago: University of Chicago Press, 1919.

TRANSLATIONS

The Twentieth Century New Testament: A Translation into Modern English. New York: Revell, 1900.

MOFFATT, JAMES. *The New Testament: A New Translation.* New York: Doran, 1914.

GOODSPEED, EDGAR J. *The New Testament: An American Translation.* Chicago: University of Chicago Press, 1923.

WEYMOUTH, R. F. *The New Testament in Modern Speech.* Revised Edition. Boston: The Pilgrim Press, 1924.

INDEX

149

PRINTED IN THE U.S.A.

"The Religion of Democracy"